Make Your Own Alterations

Simple Sewing the Professional Way

Miriam Morgan

arco
New York

To
my mother
who taught me to sew before I could walk;
to
Auntie Millie and Margaret Morrison
who unfailingly encouraged me in every undertaking,
and to
Dora Gwen Cope
whose excellent English teaching so long ago made the
writing possible,
this little book is affectionately dedicated.

Published by ARCO PUBLISHING COMPANY, Inc.
219 Park Avenue South, New York, N.Y. 10003

Second Printing, 1972

Library of Congress Catalog Number 79-96072

ISBN 0-668-02130-6

Printed in the United States of America

Contents

Introduction		5
1.	General Equipment	7
2.	About Threading Needles	9
3.	How to Sew On Buttons and Fasteners	11
	Buttons	11
	Snap Fasteners	13
	Hooks	14
4.	How to Prepare a Hem	17
	Marking	18
	Finishing Hem Edges	18
	Hem Stitches	23
5.	Shortening Skirts	27
	Shortening a Skirt with a Straight Hem	27
	Shortening a Skirt with Pleats	29
	Flared and Circular Hems	30
6.	Lengthening Skirts and Dresses	37
	Preparing the Facing	38
	Forming a New Hemline	38
	Adding a Hemband	40
	Lengthening Little Girls' Dresses	42
	Lengthening Flared and Princess Dresses	47
	Making a Suspendered Skirt from an Old Dress	50
7.	Replacing Broken Zippers	51
	How to Replace a Broken Zipper on a Skirt	51
	How to Replace a Broken Zipper on a Dress	53
	How to Replace a Side Underarm Zipper	55
8.	How to Make a Cummerbund and Scarf Set	57
9.	How to Make a Dirndl Skirt	61
	Making a Bordered Dirndl Skirt	61
10.	How to Make a Circular Skirt Without a Pattern	67
	Women's Circular Skirts	67
	Children's Circular Skirts	73

Contents (Continued)

11.	Two Ways to Make Buttonholes	77
	Bias Bound Buttonholes	77
	Straight Bound Buttonholes	79
12.	How to Refit a Tailored Skirt	81
	A Skirt that is Loose All Over	81
	A Skirt that Fits At the Top, but not Down the Sides	84
	A Skirt that Fits From the Hips Down	86
	A Skirt that Cups in Under the Seat Back	87
	A Skirt that Droops Down in the Front	89
13.	How to Refit a Dress	90
	Odds and Ends	92
	Index	94

Introduction

I HAVE written this book on sewing in hopes of helping the young housewife who wants to save time and money on family alterations and mending, the young student or business woman who wants to learn to sew in order to stretch her budget, the teenager who would like to fix her own clothes and make a few simple garments, and all who would like to sew but do not know how. Even the woman who thinks that she is "all thumbs" or who previously has tried to sew, with indifferent results, will find instructions here that, with a little application, she can follow easily.

This book will not make you into a Dior or a Mainbocher (and makes no such pretentious claims), but it does tell how to make repairs and alterations in a simple way. It will save you the time and bother of taking everything to the dressmaker, and it can save you a substantial amount of money.

You do not need a workroom full of cumbersome and expensive equipment in order to do the things described in this book. Most homes already have such things as needles, scissors and threads. In any case, the supplies and equipment used here (except for the sewing machine) can be purchased inexpensively in almost any Five-and-Ten, department store notions counter, or dressmaker supply store.

One important thing you will have to provide yourself, and that is a little *patience*. Hasty work only produces poor results. It takes a proper amount of time to produce good results. Professional work takes time as well as skill. Do not expect, as an amateur, to turn out a good job in half the time an experienced professional would take—it cannot be done.

Start with something easy. Be satisfied to do a few simple things *correctly* to begin with, and when you have the "feel" of sewing, you can try your hand at something more ambitious. Many beginners are discouraged by starting something that is too difficult.

Today sewing is the most popular hobby in the United States. More than 215 million paper patterns were sold here in 1968—proof, indeed, that many women enjoy sewing. There is immense satisfaction to be found in making something useful and beautiful, or in restoring to service something that is worn or damaged. Sewing is constructive and creative —an excellent outlet for a person with an artistic bent.

I hope this book proves to be as helpful as it is intended to be, and I wish you all joy and success in your endeavors.

MIRIAM MORGAN

1. General Equipment

You will need a table free of all clutter. For small things, such as children's clothes, a card table will do. But for adults' clothes a dining or kitchen table that is covered is best. Your work will have a better line and a more professional look if you lay it out flat on the table. You can never get straight lines on side seams, or straight hemlines if you try to work on your knees.

You must have plenty of sharp pins. It is advisable to buy a half-pound box of dressmaker's silk pins (No. 17 size is good). This all-purpose pin is sharp and smooth, and does not leave marks on the fabric. Cheap pins leave dark marks on many materials, and also make holes which cannot always be ironed out. Also they often catch on the material and pull threads. A box of good pins is a lasting and sound investment.

The right needle for the job is important. I recommend three sizes—No. 8, No. 9 and No. 10 (Long-eye Crewel Needles) for most general sewing. These are easy to thread, comfortable to hold while working, and will serve for practically any purpose.

Your scissors should be *sharp*. One pair of straight "trimmers" and one pair of small embroidery scissors are all that you need for altering and mending. If you are going to make a dress, however, a pair of bent-shank dressmaker's shears is necessary.

Keep a tape measure handy, a short ruler, a piece of chalk and several thimbles. There are many little plastic thimbles on the market that cost only a few cents, come in bright colors and are easy to find.

Of course you will need to press your work as you go, so have the iron and ironing board ready. A steam iron is good to have, but if you do not own one, then a damp cloth (free of lint and starch) can be used with your dry iron. A sleeve board is useful and convenient to have for pressing shoulders, sleeves, collars, pockets, and all sorts of odd corners. Such a board can be bought in almost all hardware stores, dressmaker supply stores, housewares, and some notions departments, and costs about two dollars. Until you get one, or when traveling, a loosely-rolled newspaper wrapped in plain paper (to keep the print from rubbing off), with a folded linen towel pinned around it, makes a good substitute.

One other useful gadget—and *well* worth its small cost—is a skirt-marker, sold in Five-and-Tens, dressmaker supply stores, and notions counters, at about two dollars. This is a great time-saver, and one of the best investments you can make. However, until you can buy one, try using a piece of chalk fastened to the leg of a chair or table with Scotch tape at the exact height you wish to make your hemline. This is a bit harder to use, as you have to have someone else press the skirt against the chalk as you turn around, but it does serve as a good substitute, and is more accurate than the pin-and-look-and-guess method.

These are the most essential items for home repairing and altering, and are usually found in most homes.

It is a good idea to keep all your sewing things in a box, so that you do not have to hunt through drawers and closets whenever you want to sew on a button. Very often, the problem of finding scissors, threads, needles, etc., discourages the beginner from attempting to do numerous small jobs that are quite easy. Frequently, by the time you have found all the needed items, there is no time left to do the job itself! All this can be avoided by the very simple method of putting *everything*—pins, needles, scissors, tape measure, chalk, ruler, thimbles, etc., in a box together. Put this box into a much larger box, in which you can keep all your threads (an assortment of colors is handy), seam-bindings, buttons, tape, elastic, mending scraps, and all the odds and ends that will accumulate as you do more jobs. By keeping everything together, your workbox will become one of your most useful and time-saving (and *money*-saving!) possessions. Also . . . and important—pins and scissors will be safely out of reach of small children.

Take care of your equipment. Do not use your sewing scissors for cutting wire, flowers, or heavy paper. Keep them *sharp*, so that you can cut thin fabrics, like chiffon, or heavy woolen cloth, without making jagged edges or uneven lines. Keep your pins and needles in boxes or a pin-cushion, or packets, where they will not rust. When in use, stick them in a cushion, not in a spool of thread, for this damages the thread and often bends the needle. A bent needle is most uncomfortable, if not impossible, to work with. Give your equipment proper care, and it will serve you long and well.

In addition to the few pieces of equipment mentioned here, you will find on the notions counters many useful gadgets. If you are gadget-minded, you may enjoy using them. However, the object of this book is to tell how you can do sewing and alterations with the least clutter and expense, so only things that are an absolute necessity are used.

For those new sewers who do not have a sewing machine, it will be helpful to know that some large department stores, and stores that sell sewing machines, have them available for rent, or for use in the store for a small hourly fee. Also hotels and clubs usually have a sewing machine in the linen room which can be used by a persuasive guest, or even rented briefly. Such places will lend an iron and ironing board, too.

So, do not feel you must buy every gadget in sight before you start to sew. You need not. To begin with, do something simple, such as a straight hem, or putting in a new zipper.

A *very* important investment is a good girdle and bra. *Always* wear good foundation garments when you go to try on or fit a new dress. A strapless bra fits quite differently from a regular one; therefore, when fitting a dress that has a strapless top, be sure to wear the correct bra. Always remember that any new foundation changes your bust, waist and hip measurements somewhat, so wear the correct one when buying or fitting a new dress.

2. About Threading Needles

MANY people dislike sewing because they have difficulty threading needles. Others buy very large, thick needles, because the eyes are larger and easier to thread, but these needles are hard to work with because they are so clumsy.

If you buy the kind of needles that are used for embroidery, called "Crewel," with long eyes, you will find that they are quite easy to thread when you do it the right way. That is, *cut* the thread; do not bite or break it. Try breaking a piece of thin string, and then look at the end. You will see that it is uneven and fuzzy, and that it curls and twists apart, even when moistened. Thread is the same, only thinner. So, *cut* your thread, slanting the scissors. Then moisten the end between your lips, pressing it flat. Hold the needle so that you can see through the eye, aim the thread gently and firmly, and it will thread without difficulty. You might practice this a few times—it will save you time later on.

Another reason it is easier to sew with thin needles is that they are easier to push through fabrics, especially if you are working on a tough or closely-woven one. A No. 10 Crewel needle will slip through "hard" fabrics, such as taffeta or chintz, whereas a thick needle is not only very hard to push through but also leaves ugly holes as it goes through, and will not make small stitches. A No. 9 Crewel is a good all-purpose needle, and will sew almost anything but the toughest fabric. A No. 8 Crewel is good for basting, or for fairly coarse wool, loose cotton weaves, denims, men's trousers, coat buttons, etc.

These needles cost about 19 cents a pack. Dressmaker supply stores carry them, and most notions counters. Surely it is worth a few cents to buy sewing comfort for a year. And unless you are very careless, three packs should last for a long time, and make your sewing much easier.

Of course, there are many other kinds of needles, many of which are fine to use. But I recommend Crewels to anyone who has difficulty threading the regular round-eye kind.

One other thing—do not buy too long a needle. Long needles are tiring to hold and bend very easily. Get them about an inch-and-a-half long if your hands are small or medium, or an inch-and-three-quarters if your hands are large. Or, try a few different sizes until you find the size that feels most comfortable. Needles should fit properly.

For basting, use a soft, cheap thread that breaks easily. This is recommended because if you baste something too tightly, in fitting, the thread will break and no harm is done to the fabric. If you use a strong thread for basting, it may cut or tear the fabric and spoil the garment. You can buy basting thread in large spools at the Five-and-Ten for a few cents.

Snap Fasteners (Figure 3-2)

Snap fasteners are meant to hold two parts of a garment together as flat as possible—and invisibly. Therefore they are sewn on as close to the fabric as possible, without a shank, or any allowance for movement.

First thread your needle, double the thread, and make a small knot. Take a tiny stitch where the center of the snap is to be. (Usually the knob or ball side of the snap is sewn on the upper side of the garment, and the bowl side of the snap on the under side of the garment). Take another tiny stitch about ¼″ away from the center, push the needle through the snap hole and slide the snap down to the garment, taking care to hold it so that the center of the snap is on the stitch which marks the center of the fastening. Now push your needle through a few threads of the material close to the snap and up through the hole in the snap. Do this three times. Slip the needle under the snap to the next hole and sew through the fabric and hole three times. Always keep your stitches close to the snap and on top of each other. Never let the stitches wander or spread out, as this allows the snap to wobble, and it soon cuts through the thread. Keep the stitches very close and tight through all four holes. When you have sewn the last hole, take three very tiny stitches on top of each other to fasten off, and clip the thread.

Close the garment, and match the other half of the snap to the opposite side. Sew it on in the same way. Your snaps will stay on for a long time if you remember to keep your stitches close, small and tight. And remember to fasten off *properly!*

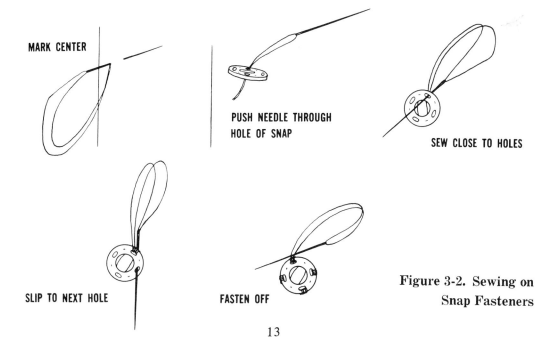

MARK CENTER

PUSH NEEDLE THROUGH HOLE OF SNAP

SEW CLOSE TO HOLES

SLIP TO NEXT HOLE

FASTEN OFF

Figure 3-2. Sewing on Snap Fasteners

Hooks (Figure 3-3)

To stay firm and secure, hooks should be sewn in three places—through the two loops at the base of the hook, and through the bend of the hook at its head.

For the hook, take a tiny stitch about ¼″ inward from the place where the garment is to close. (The size of this in-stitch will depend on the size of the hook—the larger the hook, the further in you take your stitch.) Hold the hook against the garment with the loops where your stitch is, the bend of the hook at the exact place where the garment is to close. Now take three or four stitches through the material and each loop, keeping them very small and close to the metal, not letting them spread or work loose. Slide the needle under the hook to its bend (or head) and take three or four stitches through the fabric and the hook. Fasten off firmly with three tiny, tight stitches. Always be careful not to let your stitches go through to the outside of the garment, and keep the work flat, not puckered. If the hook is sewn firmly, and fastened off properly, it will stay on until the thread wears out. Loose sewing will let the hook wobble, and that soon wears or breaks the thread, and the hook comes off. The loop (or eye) should be sewn on with small, close stitches like the ones used for hooks.

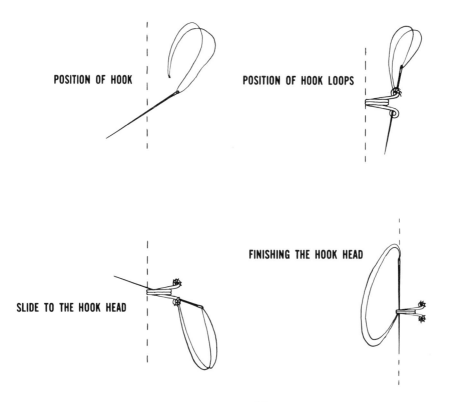

POSITION OF HOOK

POSITION OF HOOK LOOPS

SLIDE TO THE HOOK HEAD

FINISHING THE HOOK HEAD

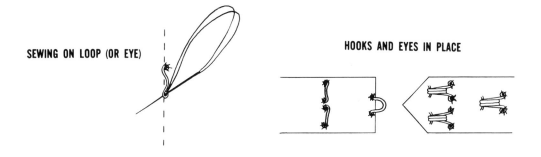

Figure 3-3. Sewing on Hooks

4. How to Prepare a Hem

THERE are many ways to hem a garment and many kinds of hems. A hem is an edge that is turned up on the wrong side of the garment and finished neatly so that it does not ravel. Hems fall into two main categories—*straight* and *curved*. Straight hems are easiest to do and are usually found on tailored skirts, sheath dresses, little girls' yoked dresses and boys' jackets. Shorts, pants, tapered skirts and shifts are variations of the straight hem. Curved hems are of many varieties: circular, flared, gored, godets, princess, etc. Curved hems are all hems that do not follow the straight or cross grain of the fabric.

Before we go on with hemming, it is important to note that there are three main cuts used in sewing. The three cuts are as follows: (Figure 4-1)

Straight Grain means the strongest or heaviest thread runs straight up and down the length of the fabric. It is called the "warp." All patterns have the straight grain marked on each piece. It is extremely important to make sure these marks are laid accurately on the straight grain of the fabric, as the "hang" of your garment depends on your accuracy.

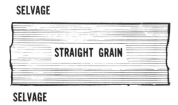

Cross Grain means the width way, or from side to side of the fabric. The threads going this way are usually thinner than those of the warp, and are called the "woof." The finished edges at the sides of the fabric are called "selvages." You often can tear fabric across the width, and this is sometimes a good way to get a straight edge before starting to cut out your garment.

Bias Cut means cut diagonally across the fabric at a 45-degree angle from the selvages. Usually a true bias is obtained by folding the material so that the cut (or torn) edge meets the selvage, forming a triangle at the end. You can never tear a bias line—it must be cut.

Never turn a hem over on itself. This makes it thick, lumpy and clumsy, and it will never hang well.

Always begin an alteration by taking out the old hem (clip the thread, do not pull it or you may damage the fabric), brush out all fuzz, and press out the old crease. If there is a pleat, press the pleat straight down.

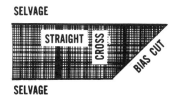

Figure 4-1. Fabric Grains

17

Marking

No matter what kind of skirt you are going to hem, one thing is always the same—it must be marked all around at an equal distance from the floor. A skirt marker is enormously helpful for this. There are several types of skirt markers on the market. My preference is the kind that blows chalk marks onto the skirt at the desired height. I recommend this kind because it is easier to use, and possibly more accurate than the clamp-and-pin variety. It is sold in Five-and-Tens and notions counters, costs about two dollars, and is a very good investment for the home sewer.

If you do not have a marker, you can use a piece of chalk Scotch-taped to the leg of a chair or table at the required height, although this is a little harder to do because someone else has to press the skirt against the chalk as you turn around. You must be very careful to stand perfectly straight and still while each mark is made. With a chalk skirt-marker, your helper can move the marker around you while you stand perfectly still. Turning around involves moving from foot to foot, and often changes one's posture and the "hang" of the skirt, resulting in an uneven chalk line.

There is no fixed "correct" length for a skirt. The proper length depends on the height of the wearer, type of skirt, current fashion, and above all, the shape of the wearer's legs. The height of the heels, and the girdle underneath, have considerable effect on the hemline, so be sure to wear the right shoes and girdle with each garment when you mark the hemline. For a start, you might measure the height of your favorite skirt from the floor, and use that as a guide. Of course, you should always pin up a hem and try it on before sewing it "for keeps," as it never hurts to make sure.

Finishing Hem Edges

The way to do a hem depends on the thickness of the fabric, the shape of the edge to be hemmed, and the type of garment. In any case, the top edge of the turned-up material forming the hem must be neatly finished. We will consider some of the ways most often used for this finishing.

Seam-binding Finish
(Figure 4-2)

Very often hems on ready-to-wear dresses are edged with seam-binding. *Seam-binding* is a narrow, straight, thin ribbon, generally 3/8" to 5/8" in width, made of silk, or rayon or nylon in many different qualities. It comes in all colors and is sold on cards, in bundles, and on rolls, from 3 yards to 100 yards. It costs from about 25 cents for a 3-yard card, to $1.25 to $1.85 for a 100-yard roll (more economical if you are doing many hems in the same color). It is not absolutely necessary for the seam-binding to match the skirt perfectly, although a good match looks best. Occasionally narrow lace edging is used instead of ribbon.

After the hem has been marked and basted up (which we will discuss later), the width of the hem is next marked. The seam-binding is laid

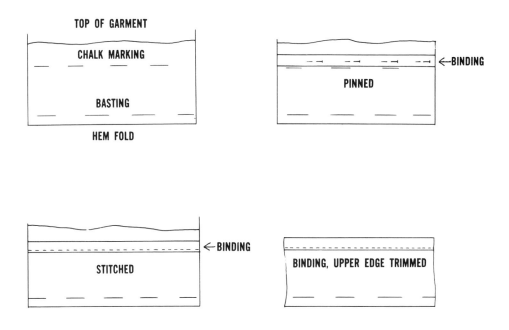

Figure 4-2. Seam-binding Finish

along the hem-allowance at the top of this line of marks, the edge of the binding just touching the marks. Then it is pinned at intervals of about 3″ all around the hem. Where the binding meets, overlap it 1″, cut off, and turn under the cut end neatly. It can then be stitched around the hem by hand or by machine. The stitching should be close to the lower edge of the seam-binding, and very even. Then any surplus material that shows above the seam-binding should be trimmed off with the trimming scissors just underneath the upper edge of the binding. It is now ready to hem.

Pinked-Edge Finish
(Figure 4-3)

Another neat finish for a hem edge, and quite practical for materials that do not ravel (such as felt, glazed chintz, some flannel, tightly woven wools and cottons, etc.) is a pinked edge. This is quickly and easily done by cutting the hem-allowance along the marked line with pinking shears. *Pinking shears* are heavy shears with zig-zag blades, which cut an even zig-zagged edge. They cost about $3.95 and up, and it pays to buy good ones.

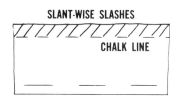

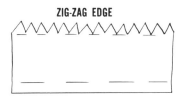

Figure 4-3. Pinked-Edge Finish

If you do not have any pinking shears, you can pink with straight scissors, only it takes a little more time and care. You do it the following way: First mark your hem-allowance all around with chalk, making the marks almost continuous. Then trim off all excess material ¼″ *above* this line of marks. Now with the tips of your scissors, cut tiny slant-wise slashes all around the edge in one direction about ⅜″ to ½″ apart, ending each slash at the chalk line. Turn the skirt around, and do the same thing again in the opposite direction, starting each slash at the top of a slash, and ending at the bottom of the next slash. As you go, tiny triangles of material will fall away, leaving a nice, neat zig-zag edge, all ready to hem.

Stitch-and-Overcast Edge
(Figure 4-4)

Probably the best finish of all, and the one used by the French design houses and all fine custom dressmakers, is the stitch-and-overcast edge. It is done as follows: A line of stitches (hand or machine) is run along the line marking the hem width. The surplus material is then

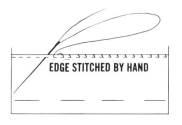

Figure 4-4.
Stitch-and-Overcast Edge

trimmed off to about ⅛″ above the stitch line edges. The edge is stitched all around, by hand, each stitch starting on the wrong side of the material and coming through to the right side, so that the thread goes over the edge of the fabric, with each stitch. The stitches should be quite small, not larger than ¼″ apart, and not pulled too tight, or the edge will be puckered. When it has been *overcast* (as this is called) all around, it is pressed, and then it is ready to finish. This is not at all difficult to do, it just takes a little time. It is a really fine finish to any good garment.

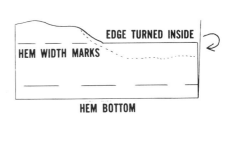

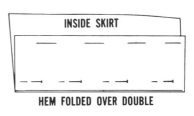

Figure 4-5. Turned-in Edge

A Turned-in Edge (Figure 4-5)

Very thin fabrics, such as chiffon, voile, China silk, batiste, dimity, etc., can be turned in along the line of hem-width marks, pressed flat and trimmed evenly inside. If a firm edge is desired at the top of the hem, it can be stitched by machine or by hand along the pressed fold. This is often necessary if the fabric is crease-resistant, to keep the edge flat. Sometimes when the material is sheer, the turned-in fabric is left wide enough to come to the bottom of the hem, and cut even with the fold of the hem. This looks nice, because you do not have two thicknesses at the bottom of the hem and three at the top, but the same three thicknesses all through the hem. If there is not enough material to do this, then the top must be trimmed very evenly inside the fold, as it will probably show through a little.

Bias Binding a Hem Edge (Figure 4-6)

Sometimes hem edges are bound with bias binding. This is harder to do, but looks nice when carefully done. It is a finish generally used on men's and women's overcoats, very thick fabrics, and sportswear.

Bias binding is thin silk, cotton, or rayon, cut on the bias in narrow strips, with both edges turned toward each other and pressed. It comes in all colors—on cards, bundles, and by-the-yard—in Five-and-Tens, notions counters, and dressmaker supply stores, and costs only a few cents.

To bind a hem edge, first mark the hem width. Then with the cut edges facing up (folded side to the fabric), lay the binding along the line of marks with the top fold on the marks. Open the top fold (lift it up) and pin the binding all around the hem. Cut off when it overlaps and turn in the cut underneath end neatly. Stitch the binding in the fold where you have the pins (by hand or machine) then press it up over the stitching. Cut off any excess hem material under the binding about $\frac{1}{8}''$ from the stitches. Turn the bias binding over the hem edge, and slip-stitch or hem it to the stitching line. Press firmly, and it is ready to finish.

This bound edge is also used to finish the facings in unlined jackets, seams in unlined coats, and bathrobes. It is a good firm finish and will last a long time.

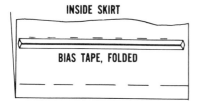

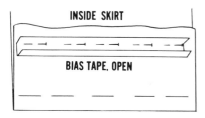

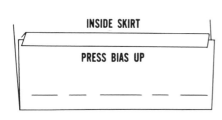

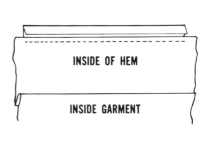

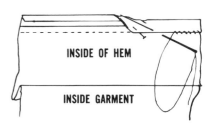

Figure 4-6. Binding a Hem Edge

Hem Stitches (Figure 4-7)

There are many different ways of stitching up a hem. Your choice will depend on the thickness and weight of the material and on which stitch you find easiest to do.

The most generally used stitch is called "hemming." This covers stitches of all sizes, and is a stitch taken in the fabric, one through the seam-binding (or edge), then another stitch in the fabric, and another in the seam-binding, and so on. In our grandmother's day, when clothes had to last until they wore to pieces, it was customary to hem with tiny tight stitches. But with the advent of the sewing machine and cheaper ready-made clothes, this went out of fashion. Nowadays the best hem is the one that shows least. For a good hem in a wool or silk dress, a stitch about $\frac{3}{8}''$ to $\frac{1}{2}''$ long is advisable. That will hold up an average hem securely, and it is easy to do and goes quickly.

Start by taking two tiny stitches on top of each other at a side seam. Now, about $\frac{1}{2}''$ away (sewing toward the left if you are right-handed, towards the right if you are left-handed), pick up two or three threads on the back of the skirt material. Do not push the needle through the fabric to the other side or the stitch will show. Use a *thin* needle, and you will soon get the knack of picking up a thread or two. Then pick up the *very edge* of the seam-binding. Pull the thread through until it lies flat on the edge of the seam-binding, almost straight. Your stitching will be neater if you try to hold your needle almost straight along (or parallel with) the edge of the seam-binding, and pick up threads of the fabric just underneath or right alongside of the binding. Do not let your needle turn at a sharp angle to the hem, or wander far away from the binding. The stitches should be pulled flat, but not tight, as you go.

Some people like to take an occasional back-stitch every now and then, to make it stronger. But I do not advise this, for these reasons: if by any chance you catch your heel in the hem, the hem will not give way, but may possibly trip you up. If the hem is not back-stitched, the thread will pull, probably break, and the hem will come down, releasing the heel, and is less likely to trip you. Also a hem that is back-stitched to hold too strongly will hold if it catches on anything, and often results in a torn skirt; whereas, if the thread is loose enough to pull out, the hem will come out, and no damage is done to the fabric.

Another way to stitch up a hem, often used for thick fabrics and pinked or overcast edges, is a catch stitch. This is done by folding back the top edge of the hem-allowance, about a quarter of an inch, and alternately catching up a few threads of the skirt fabric, then a few threads in the hem-allowance fold, back and forth all around. This makes a very nice hem, and the stitches are invisible.

A hem finish often used for jersey or stretchy fabrics is a cross stitch. This is done by sewing backward. First pick up a few threads on the skirt fabric, needle pointed toward your left hand, then take a stitch in the hem-allowance about $\frac{1}{4}''$ from the edge, and about $\frac{3}{4}''$ back (or toward the right hand (1). This will make a slanting stitch from the skirt

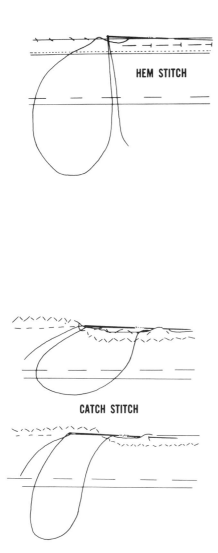

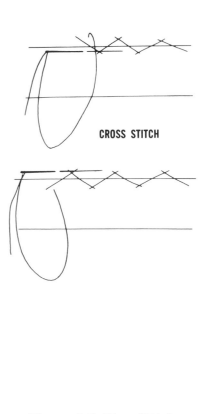

Figure 4-7. Hem Stitches

to the hem, the thread passing over the hem edge. Now pick up a few more threads in the skirt fabric $\frac{1}{4}''$ to the right, then another stitch in the hem-allowance $\frac{3}{4}''$ back. This will form a cross stitch, which is flexible, and will give slightly if the jersey stretches. It is quite easy to do, once you get the hang of it. It takes a little more time than straight hemming, but is the best hem for all stretchy fabrics. A large cross stitch is often used for coat hems inside linings, or for very bulky materials, and for catching back facings inside a coat.

When you want to do a hem, give yourself enough time. This way you can relax, and avoid getting tense and nervous. Do not try to do it in a hurry, or you will not do a very good job. For a straight tailored skirt about 45″ around, allow *at least* an hour-and-a-half to two hours—to rip, brush, press, mark, pin, edge-finish, hem, and press. This is a job that usually costs about five dollars or more at a good tailor's or dressmaker's, so it is worth the time it takes.

As you gain experience, you will gain speed. If you are doing two or three skirts at the same time, you will learn to do all the ripping at once, all the pressing at the same time, all the trying-on and marking at one session, all the machining in one swoop, and all the finishing and pressing at one go. It does not take much longer to do three or four hems at once, than to do two separately. And think of the money you can save in just one evening!

5. Shortening Skirts

Shortening a Skirt with a Straight Hem (Figure 5-1)

LET us start with a straight tailored skirt that needs shortening. First clip the hemming stitches around the old hem, turn the hem down, brush away any fuzz or lint, and press out the old crease.

Next adjust your skirt marker to the new height you want the hem to be. Put the skirt on, and make sure it is properly fastened and is quite straight at the back and front, and side seams. Stand with both feet together and keep perfectly still while your helper moves the marker around you—blowing little marks every few inches. The slit of the marker through which the chalk is blown should touch the skirt each time, so that the marks are clear and sharp.

Then take off the skirt and lay it on the table, right-side out, hem toward you. Fold back the top part and turn up the hem of the lower part along the line of chalk marks, starting at the center-front or center-back. Always put pins in at right angles to the fold, not along the fold. The new hemline should be quite straight along the front and back centers, but it may rise or drop very slightly at the sides, depending on the shape of the wearer's hips. Do not worry if the two sides are not exactly alike; many people have uneven hips, and one skirt side may be slightly longer than the other, but will look straight at the hemline when it is worn. Straighten out any slight unevenness or bumps so that you have a smooth line all around. Try the skirt on and be sure that you have the length that you like, and that it looks straight. If it is still too long or short, trace the hemline you have just made with colored thread, then measure up or down with a ruler, from the traced line, and baste. Try it on again before sewing.

Then baste around the hemline about half an inch from the fold, keeping the turned-up material very flat, especially at the center-front and back.

Take your short ruler and with chalk or pins make a row of marks about 2″ or 2½″ from the fold of the new hemline (2″ to 3″ is a standard good width for most hems).

At this point you must decide what kind of finish you will use for the top of your new hem: seam-binding, overcast, pinking, etc.

Finish the top edge of your hem, press and pin up all around. Finally take your needle (a No. 9 Crewel), thread it with single thread and, starting at a side seam, take a tiny stitch in the seam. With the skirt toward you, hold the hem in the left hand, with the hem held between the thumb and first finger. Open the first and second fingers, pull the hem across them, and hold it between the second and third fingers. Now if the top of the hem is finished with seam-binding, hold the needle along the

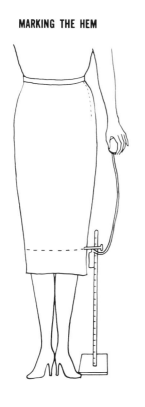

MARKING THE HEM

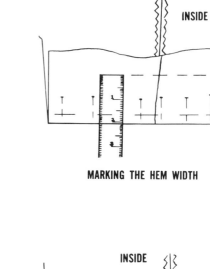

INSIDE

MARKING THE HEM WIDTH

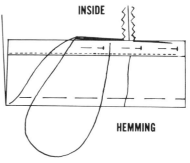

INSIDE

HEMMING

**Figure 5-1. Shortening a Straight
Tailored Skirt**

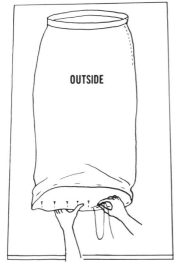

OUTSIDE

BASTING THE HEM

seam-binding parallel to it and pick
up a thread or two of the skirt fabric, making sure not to let the stitch
go right through to the outside. Pull
the thread through until it lies flat,
then catch the edge of the seam-binding and pull through. Now pick up a
few threads of the skirt about half an
inch forward, pick up the edge of the
binding, and pull through again. Re-
peat all around, then fasten off securely. Do not pull the thread too
tight, or it will show a line of puckers
on the outside. Press the whole skirt
as well as the hem, and it is finished.

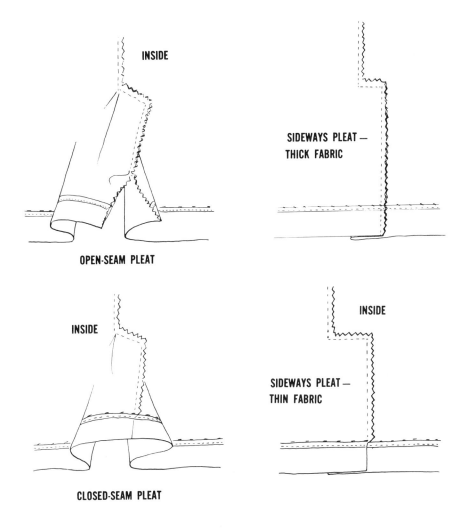

INSIDE

OPEN-SEAM PLEAT

SIDEWAYS PLEAT — THICK FABRIC

INSIDE

CLOSED-SEAM PLEAT

SIDEWAYS PLEAT — THIN FABRIC

INSIDE

Figure 5-2. Shortening a Skirt with Pleat

Shortening a Skirt with Pleats (Figure 5-2)

A great many skirts are made with pleats in the side or center-back. If the material is fairly thick, or there is a seam down the inner edge of the pleat, it is generally better to hem the bottom of the skirt with the pleat-seam undone then to stitch through the hem double. Trim and overcast the raw edges together. This way the back of the pleat is thinner and flat-ter, and the pleat keeps its crease much better. Of course, if the material is very thin, then the pleat seam can be sewn all the way down, the seam pressed open, and the hem carried right across it. Then it is pressed double on the seam, with the seam-allowance clipped at the top of the hem.

Flared and Circular Hems (Figure 5-3)

Skirts that are cut in several sections so that there is more material at the hem than at the top are called *flared* (or gored). *Circular* skirts are cut in one large circle (if the fabric is wide enough) or with a seam on each side, and a hole in the center for the waist. *Semi-circular* skirts are cut in a half circle, and generally have a center-back seam and zipper. *Godets* (pronounced "go-days") are triangular pieces of material set in the lower part of a skirt to add fullness at the bottom, lower part of the triangle curved at the hem.

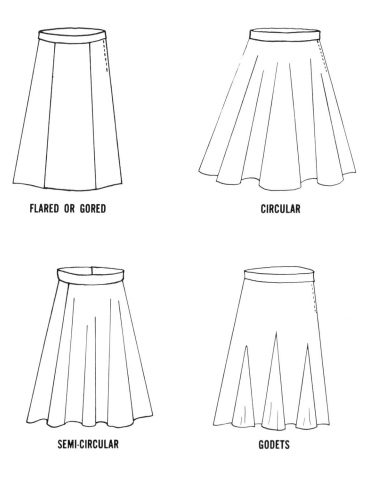

FLARED OR GORED   CIRCULAR

SEMI-CIRCULAR   GODETS

Figure 5-3. Flared and Circular Hems

Eliminating Fullness from Flared Hem (Figure 5-4)

When you hem a flared or circular skirt, there is always a certain amount of extra fullness in the turned-up hem-allowance. In some fabrics, such as soft woolens, this excess can be shrunk or steam-pressed out so that the hem will lie flat all around. But other fabrics such as satins, taffetas, glazed cottons—will not shrink, so this extra fullness must be carefully pleated out.

Let us first consider a flared or circular hem, fairly full, in a soft woolen fabric. Follow the first steps: rip, press and mark hemline as for straight hems. Then lay your skirt flat on the table, right-side out, hem toward you. Turn up the hem inside along the line of chalk marks, putting your pins in at right angles to the fold, and close to the fold. Then baste along the fold about ¼" up. Now mark a line for the hem width, about 2" or 2½" up. Put in a row of small running stitches all around this

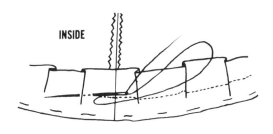

GATHERING TOP OF CIRCULAR OR FLARED HEM

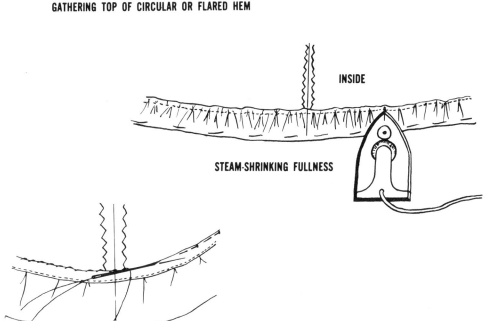

STEAM-SHRINKING FULLNESS

HEMMING CIRCULAR SKIRT

Figure 5-4. Eliminating Fullness
From Flared Hem

31

line. Put the skirt on the ironing board, and pull up the thread so that the fullness is drawn up until the hem-allowance is slightly gathered. Steam press this very lightly, using the tip of the iron to work out the gathered fullness. Do this all around until all (or most) of the fullness has disappeared and the hem-allowance lies flat. Re-mark the hem-width, as shrinking and pressing may have made your first line uneven. Finish your top-edge (you will have to decide which is the best finish to use, depending on the fabric). Press again, then sew up your hem. If you have finished it with seam-binding, and the material is fairly thin, a slip-stitch is the best finish, as on the straight skirt. The procedure is the same for circular and godet hems except that there is generally more fullness to be steamed or pleated out of the hem allowance.

Pleating Out Fullness of Hem
(Figure 5-5)

If your fabric is one that will not shrink, it is done slightly differently. But first, rip out the old hem, brush and press as before. Put on the skirt and mark your new hemline with chalk, making the marks fairly close together; and be sure you mark inside any folds (this is important in circular and godet hems) and on all seams. Then take off the skirt and pin it up along the new hemline; pins should be at right angles and close to the folded edge, as before. Baste.

Now this is where we do it somewhat differently. Instead of shrinking out the fullness, it must be taken out in tiny pleats. Lay your skirt flat on the table, hem toward you. Fold back the top half, and mark the hem width all around. Do not try to make too wide a hem on a circular skirt,

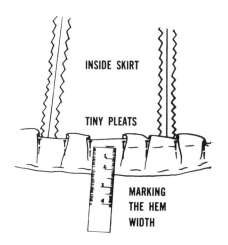

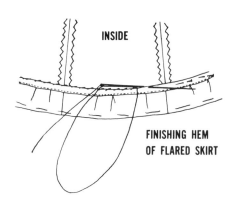

Figure 5-5. Pleating Out Fullness of Hem

especially if you are a beginner. About 1″ or 1½″ will be wide enough. When pressing a hem up, it is a good idea to put a piece of thick paper or cloth inside the hem-allowance to prevent pressing the hemline through to the right side.

When you have marked your hem width all around, trim off any excess material ½″ above this line. Be very careful to turn the hem-allowance up evenly, pin in tiny pleats wherever there is extra fullness, so that the top of the hem, where you just put that line of chalk marks, lies as flat as possible (it will not lie quite flat until it is pressed) on the skirt. Baste around, catching each pleat into place. Press this gently, on a thick, soft ironing-board. You can put a folded terry cloth towel under the regular ironing-board cover to make a soft surface. Do not press hard, or you will press the pleats into the outside of the skirt, and they will show through. If you accidentally press some pleats through, loosen the basting, lift the hem, and press underneath the hem allowance until the marks disappear. But it is much easier to be careful and not press too heavily!

After you have pressed the pleats in, you must decide which finish to use for the hem edge. It is easiest to put on a seam-binding unless the material is extremely thick; or else do a hand-overcast edge. This takes time, especially on a very full hem, but it is easy.

If you decide to put on a seam-binding, there are two ways to sew it on. You can stitch the seam-binding on flat along the hem-width marks right over the pleats, or you can stitch it on flat, opening each pleat as you go, and repressing them

(with the seam-binding as well) before hemming. Either way is alright —do whichever you find easier. It will probably depend on whether you are doing it by hand or machine and on how thick your material is. Then hem it.

Do not try to put seam-binding on velvet if you are a beginner. It is very difficult to keep it straight, even when doing it by hand. Turn the velvet ones over to a dressmaker, or do a hand-overcast edge, keeping the stitches small.

Machined-Edge Hems
(Figure 5-6)

If the circular skirt you are going to hem is a casual or play skirt of some type, of denim or some kind of firm cotton, then the best hem is the machined edge. To do this, follow the usual steps of taking out the old hem, brushing, and pressing flat, then marking the new hemline with chalk.

Pin up the new hem along the chalk line, pins at right angles and close to the fold. Baste around, about ½″ from the fold, easing any fullness. Press.

You can either do your hem with matching thread or, if you feel inclined to use a decorative finish, use a contrasting thread—red on blue, or white on red, or match one of your accessory colors.

Thread up your machine, and stitch around the hem very close to the fold—about ⅛″ from the edge— being careful to keep the stitching line very even. It does not matter whether you stitch on the inside or the outside of the skirt as long as your machine stitch is the same on

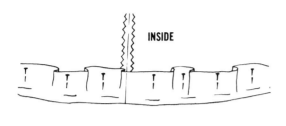

INSIDE

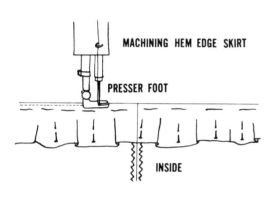

MACHINING HEM EDGE SKIRT

PRESSER FOOT

INSIDE

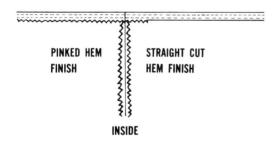

PINKED HEM
FINISH

STRAIGHT CUT
HEM FINISH

INSIDE

Figure 5-6. Machine-edged Hems

both sides. Usually it is easier to stitch on the inside, as you can hold the hem fullness in place better. Stitch it around a second time, using the presser-foot as a guide, the second row of stitching a presser-foot width above the first line. If you can control the hem fullness easily, it looks nice to have a third line of stitching, but this is not necessary. When the stitching is done, take your pinking shears and trim off the excess material inside, keeping the pinking ¼″ above the stitching. Then press, and it is done.

If you have no pinking shears, you can pink by hand with ordinary scissors, or just trim off with straight scissors, as long as the material does not ravel too freely. Be careful not to cut too close to the stitching line and clip into the hem.

This is a good, quick finish for children's play clothes that are nearly worn out and will not need letting down any more. It is firm and neat, does not pull out, and takes hardly any time to do. It is a good finish for overalls, aprons, denim pants, and all casual clothes used for rough wear.

For a circular skirt of silk or wool that needs an invisible hem, a fairly narrow hem edged with seam-binding is best. Follow the usual first steps: take out the old hem, brush, press, and mark closely all around with chalk. Turn up along the new hemline, with the skirt flat on the table, pins at right angles to the fold. Baste about ½″ above the fold, then press lightly, pressing out as much fullness as possible. Mark the new hem-width, about ¾″ to 1″. Pin seam-binding around the hem along this line, being very careful not to stretch the skirt material, and easing in any hem fullness stitch. Press flat as possible (do not press hard enough to make the hem show through on the right side). Pin up, and slip-stitch the hem. If there is any extra fullness, you can take in tiny pleats now and then, but do not sew them down very hard, as this will make puckers on the outside. Rather, sew them loosely, and let the pressing hold them.

When a skirt is made full by means of inset godets, the extra hem fullness will come right in the godets. In this case, the hem fullness is pleated out only in the godets, the straight part of the skirt hem being turned up flat, the godet seams turned up straight upon themselves.

For this reason, it is just as well to make this kind of hem rather narrow, as that leaves less fullness to be pleated. After the hem has been turned up, pinned, and basted near the fold, mark the hem-width about $\frac{1}{2}''$ up from the fold, and set on the seam-binding. With the seam-binding set just above the $\frac{1}{2}''$ marks, this will give you a hem about an inch wide, which is enough on this kind of skirt. Slip-stitch with rather small stitches on the curved parts, so that the weight of the pleated hem does not make it sag at the godets. Press carefully, again being cautious not to press the pleats through to mark the right side of the skirt.

6. Lengthening Skirts and Dresses

IN this chapter we will consider how to lengthen certain garments and how to face hems. Of course, if you have a skirt with a very wide hem, you can let it down in the same way you have been raising hems—that is, rip, press and brush, mark, pin, edge-finish and hem. However, if there is not enough material left below the new length marks for hem-allowance, you have a choice of either making a very narrow hem, or facing it up. Usually a skirt hangs better if there is something to give the hem a little weight. Many hems are faced, which means that a piece of material has been sewn on the bottom of the skirt and turned up to form a hem 2" or 3" wide.

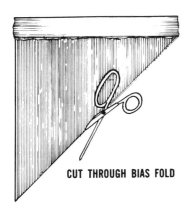

CUT THROUGH BIAS FOLD

MARK WIDTH

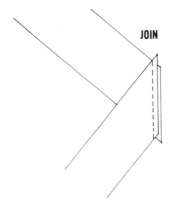

JOIN

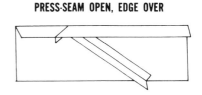

PRESS-SEAM OPEN, EDGE OVER

Figure 6-1. Preparing the Facing

Preparing the Facing (Figure 6-1)

Most skirts are faced the following way: regardless of their shape or fullness. First buy a piece of material in some fairly thin fabric (rayon taffeta is excellent for this) in a yard goods store. Or, if you can buy the right color, get a package of bias binding 2" wide in the notions department—this saves work and time. If you have to buy material, get ¾ yard, fold diagonally (cut and folded to selvage), pat it flat, and cut through the fold. Now you have two triangles of taffeta. With your chalk and ruler, mark 3" from the cut edges, and cut (through both pieces) two long bias strips, 3" wide. Join the pieces at the selvages making a diagonal seam when the material is opened. Press seam open, and press one edge of this strip over into a ½" fold.

Forming a New Hemline (Figure 6-2)

Mark the new hemline with your skirt marker, turn the skirt inside out, and lay it on the table, upper part pushed back. Pin and baste the new hem. Put your pins and basting close to the fold. Now, on the turn-up, put a line of chalk marks all around the skirt ½" above the new hemline. (If you do not have a ½" turned up, make the line as high as you can, getting it even all around.) You do this by measuring it at the narrowest spot, and using that for your measurement. (If you have more than ½", you can make this line a bit higher, which is all to the good.) If you are using ready-made bias binding, you can either put it on the hem just as you stitched on straight seam-binding, pinning it on top of your chalk line, and stitching close to the lower edge, or you can open it as you did for bias binding an edge, pin it inside the upper fold, and stitch along inside the fold of the bias facing. This way the stitching will not show.

If you are using cut fabric strips, you pin the bias strip on the skirt turn-up along the chalk line, with the ½" pressed fold as your guide. You can either stitch it on the outside fold-edge, like seam-binding, or you can stitch it inside the fold, so that the stitches will not show. When you have your facing sewn on, you press it up, flat against the skirt. Now, take your ruler, and mark the hem-width you desire—2", 2½", 3" from the hemline fold; turn in the taffeta at this line, and press again. Put in some pins while you have it flat on the ironing board, and it is ready to hem.

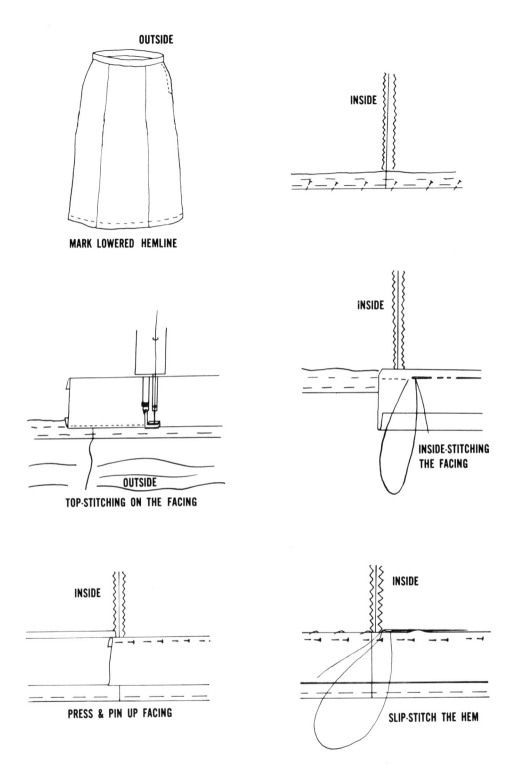

OUTSIDE

MARK LOWERED HEMLINE

INSIDE

INSIDE

TOP-STITCHING ON THE FACING

OUTSIDE

INSIDE

INSIDE-STITCHING
THE FACING

INSIDE

PRESS & PIN UP FACING

INSIDE

SLIP-STITCH THE HEM

Figure 6-2. Forming New Hemline

39

Adding a Hemband (Figure 6-3)

When a skirt just is not long enough, even with the old hem pressed out, the only way to lengthen it is to add something to it. If you can match the material exactly (which is not very often), you can set on a bias band all around, and this often looks very nice.

If you cannot get the same fabric, sometimes a band of different material in the same color looks nice—a satin hem on a wool dress, or a velvet hem on a silk dress.

To put a satin band on a skirt hem, first mark your skirt at an even line all around with the skirt marker. Baste around this line with a bright thread, so that it is easy to see, in case the chalk comes out in handling.

Let us suppose you want to make your skirt three inches longer than the line you have just marked. Fold your satin diagonally, cut through the fold, and pin the edges so that they are even. This is pinned because the satin is slippery and may not stay together when you start to cut. You might put pins here and there, just to keep it even. Now, the simplest way to make this border is to cut a piece of satin twice as wide as the border is to be (say 6″ for a 3″ border,) *plus* turnings (1″ for two sides, ½″ each), fold it in half, right-sides out, press, and baste ½″ from the cut edges—being *very* careful not to let the satin twist or slip. Then, with the cut edges toward the bottom of the skirt, fold upward, pin the satin onto the outside of the skirt with the border bastings on the bright thread line, patting the bias

band gently, to keep it easy, and not stretched or pulled. Baste all around keeping a few pins in the border above the sewing line, to prevent twisting.

Where the band ends meet (and this should be at a side or center-back seam), overlap 1″ and cut off any excess material. Undo the bastings a little way on both sides of this join, open the bias band. Put the edges together (right sides of the fabric facing each other) and make a ½″ seam. Press open, refold the bias band, and baste to the skirt.

An alternative, and better way to join up the band which takes a little more thought, is to measure the width of the skirt hem, add about 2″ (to allow for the curve around the hemline) and cut the bias band this size, cutting on the straight grain at both ends, then joining these ends, forming a circle. Press open, then fold the bias band in half, and set on as above. Then you sew it, either by hand or machine, along the basting line, stitching through both thicknesses of satin as well as through the skirt. Remove all bastings, and press the border downward. Trim off any uneven material inside, and finish the raw edges either with a hand over-casting, or pinking. If you want to tie in the border to some other part of the dress, you might add a satin bow at the neck, or make a satin belt, or make satin buttons (you can get button forms in Five-and-Ten cent stores, all ready to use and quite easy to cover).

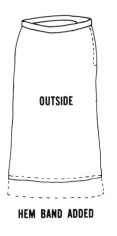

HEM BAND ADDED

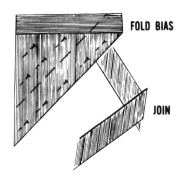

FOLD BIAS

JOIN

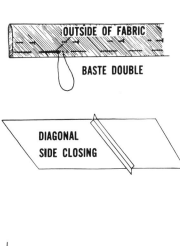

OUTSIDE OF FABRIC

BASTE DOUBLE

DIAGONAL
SIDE CLOSING

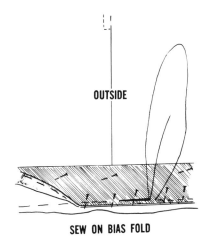

OUTSIDE

SEW ON BIAS FOLD

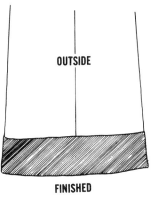

OUTSIDE

FINISHED

Figure 6-3. Adding a Hem Band

41

Lengthening Little Girls' Dresses (Figure 6-4)

Many little girls' dresses are made with straight, full skirts gathered onto yokes or fitted bodices. Usually they have a fair amount of material in the hem to allow for growth. Let us consider how to let one of these dresses down, without showing the worn marks of the old hemline.

Start as usual by clipping the hem-stitches, being very careful not to make any holes. Then brush out the fuzz, and press flat.

Turn up the hem-allowance $\frac{1}{4}''$ *above* the line where the old hemline was. Baste. Sew along the old hemline by hand or machine. If you want to make it decorative, you might do this in embroidery thread of contrasting color, keeping your hand stitches very even. This makes a tuck $\frac{1}{4}''$ deep. Press the hem-allowance and tuck down flat.

Next take your ruler, and pin or chalk a line of dots on the outside $\frac{1}{2}''$ above the stitches at the top of the tuck you have just made. Fold skirt up inside the dress along this line, baste and stitch around as close to the edge (or fold) as you can, keeping the stitches very even. This makes a tiny tuck, called a "pin-tuck" because it is only about as wide as a pin. Press the hem-allowance and the pin-tuck down.

Make another line of dots $\frac{3}{4}''$ below the *stitches* of the large ($\frac{1}{4}''$) tuck; turn up the hem-allowance and baste, stitch along the edge as before, to make another pin-tuck. Press hem-allowance and pin tuck downward. Then using your model, pin the front of the dress the length you want it to be. Remove the dress.

Turn up the hem evenly all around, using the front part you have just pinned as your guide. Finish the hem with a fairly small slip-stitch, press and you are finished.

Once you have tried your hand at tuck-trimming a skirt, you will find you can make all sorts of variations on this for many dresses. If you have a modern machine that makes fancy stitches, you can put rows of machine embroidery around the skirt, or even cover the old hemline with a fancy stitch instead of a tuck, or you can sew on a few rows of ric-rac, which you can find in the Five-and-Ten. But tuck-trimming is quick and easy, once you get the knack of it, and it does not involve buying anything or matching anything except thread. And it can be done by hand. It is used a great deal on babies' clothes and lingerie for trimming.

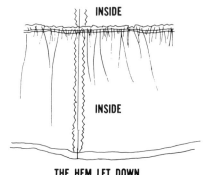

THE HEM LET DOWN

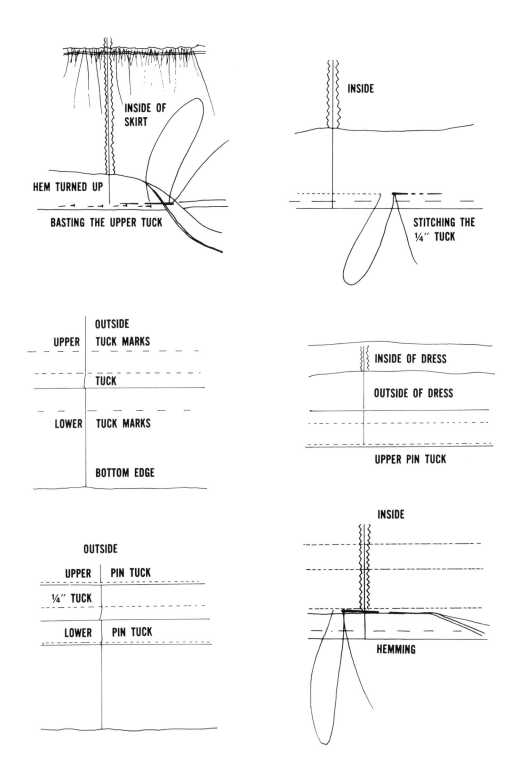

Figure 6-4. How to Lengthen Little Girls' Dresses

43

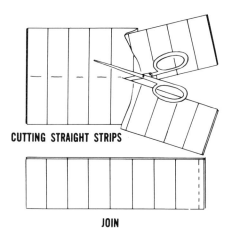

CUTTING STRAIGHT STRIPS

JOIN

Putting On a False Hem
(Figure 6-5)

Suppose you want to let down a dress and there is only enough material in the original hem to make the dress longer, but not enough for a hem. In this case, you must face up the dress with a false hem. It is not hard to do, if you do it step-by-step and allow sufficient time.

You can either match the material in its own color or, on some dresses, a hem-facing of contrasting or printed fabric can be rather effective. If the dress is straight-skirted and full, you can use a straight-grain piece of fabric for facing.

Suppose you are letting down a navy blue dress with a straight full

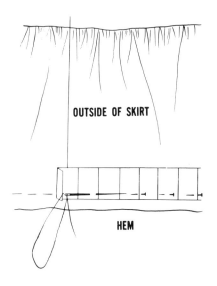

OUTSIDE OF SKIRT

HEM

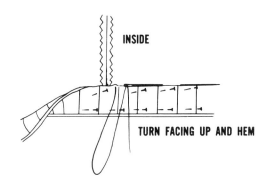

INSIDE

TURN FACING UP AND HEM

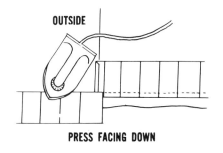

OUTSIDE

PRESS FACING DOWN

Figure 6-5. Putting On a False Hem

skirt. You might buy ¼ yard of red and blue striped cotton for the facing. Cut or tear (only tear, if it is torn when you buy it—otherwise it may be cut crookedly, and will be too small when torn straight) into strips 3″ wide. Join.

Pin the facing all around the hem on the outside of the dress, an even distance from the old hemline. (If the dress has stretched, or hangs crookedly, it is better to put it on and mark it with a chalk marker.) Put the right side of the facing to the right side of the dress, and allow ½″ for turnings. Stitch, by hand or machine, all around. Press flat, pressing the seam and facing downward.

Now turn up this facing all around inside the skirt, on the seam you have just made, taking care that the facing does not fold or show on the outside. Baste. Overlap 1″ and turn in at the side. Turn in the top of the hem-allowance if it is thin material (overcast if it is thick) and slip-stitch around the hem. Press on a thick-padded ironing board, making sure you do not press the hem hard enough to show on the outside.

Putting On a Border
(Figure 6-6)

If a dress is too short, and does not have enough hem-allowance inside to lengthen it, then it is necessary to add a border. Take the dress to a yard goods store, and find a decorative material (if the dress is made of plain fabric) that looks pretty with it. If it is a printed dress, find a plain material that matches one of the colors in the print. Get a material that is about the same weight or

thickness as the material of the dress, or else a little thinner. Do not buy thick material for a hem or border.

To make a straight border for a dress two yards around if the border is to be 2″ deep, you will need ¼ yard of 36″ to 39″ fabric. If the dress is fuller, or if you want the border wider, you will need ⅜ or ½ yard. Remember we are going to make this border out of double material, so figure 4″ for the 2″ border, *plus* ½″ for small turnings, 2 strips for a two-yard skirt. If you need a 3″ border, you must figure 6″ for the border, ½″ for turnings, 2 strips, making 13″, or ⅜ yard. If the skirt is more than 2 yards around, you need more strips, or wider material. This is where the sales clerk should be able to help you. Be sure to buy enough.

Now that the material is bought and the dress pressed and ready, we can begin. Cut or tear your border material into strips *twice* the width the border is to be, *plus* an allowance for seams. If it is firm cotton, or something thin that does not ravel, a ¼″ seam-allowance *on each side* will be enough—½″ altogether. If it is soft or loose in weave, allow at least ½″ seam on each side—1″ altogether. Join the strips at the selvage, right sides together. Press the seams open, then fold the long strip in half, right-side out, and press again. Pin at intervals, to hold the edges together. It is easier to keep it flat if you pin it while it is flat on the ironing board.

Now pin this double strip around the skirt along the bottom where the old hem-edge used to be, using the old line as a guide. You lay the border on the dress, the fold upward on the outside of the dress, and pin the border ¼″ or ½″ (depending on how

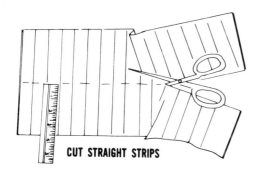

CUT STRAIGHT STRIPS

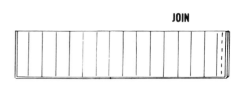

JOIN

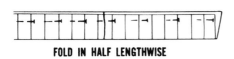

FOLD IN HALF LENGTHWISE

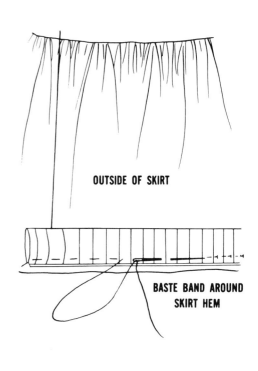

OUTSIDE OF SKIRT

BASTE BAND AROUND SKIRT HEM

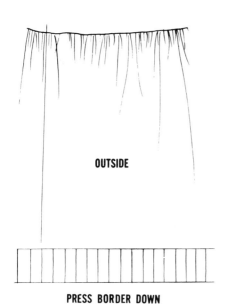

OUTSIDE

PRESS BORDER DOWN

Figure 6-6. Putting On a Border

much you allowed for the seam) from the cut edges. Baste this all around, being careful to keep the border flat without twists and puckers anywhere. When you have basted all around and the border meets, overlap it 1″ and cut off surplus. Then clip the basting on each side of this place, open up the border, and make a ½″ seam inside.

Press the seam open (you can do this with your thumb-nail), put the border edge together again, and baste the border into position. It is ready to machine or hand sew. Press down, and it is done.

Lengthening Flared and Princess Dresses (Figure 6-7)

If the dress you are lengthening is flared, princess or circular, you will need a bias border. This takes a little more material, as you have to cut your strips diagonally. About ¾ yard or 1 yard is enough for almost any dress but the very fullest kind. For a child's dress, ¾ yard should be enough.

Follow the same procedure as before—rip old hem, press, mark an even line around the skirt, and decide how wide you want the border to be. Figure twice the border width, plus a ½″ allowance for each side seam (1″ for both sides). Fold your material diagonally (cut end to selvage) and cut through the fold. Pin here and there, to hold the two triangles together. With chalk or pins, mark the width you want for the border strips and cut on the bias. Join, right sides together, at the selvages. Press seam open.

Now measure the bottom of the skirt around the edge where you are going to attach the border. Measure carefully, for your border must fit properly. Now measure the border strip, starting at the tip of one diagonal end. Allow 1″ for turnings, and 1″ for "ease," and mark this point. Cut across this end, slanting the cut in the same direction as the diagonal end from which you measured. Put these ends together right sides facing (they will be at right-angles to each other) and join. Open and press. Now fold the border in half lengthwise, and press. You now have a complete circle just a fraction wider than the bottom of the skirt. Put pins in at the half-way and quarter-way. Mark the center-front and center-back of the skirt, and the half-way in between. (This may or may not be the side seam—some dresses are fuller in front than back, and vice-versa.) Mark all four quarters evenly. Turn dress inside out, lay flat on table.

Now with the seams in the border at the back part of the dress, pin the border all around the bottom of the dress, with the fold up, right side of border on the right side of the dress,

PRINCESS DRESS

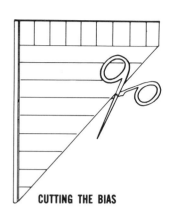

CUTTING THE BIAS

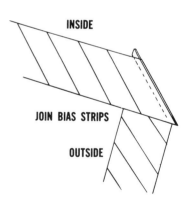

INSIDE

JOIN BIAS STRIPS

OUTSIDE

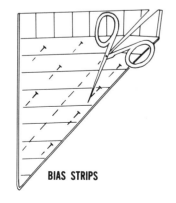

BIAS STRIPS

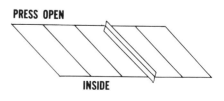

PRESS OPEN

INSIDE

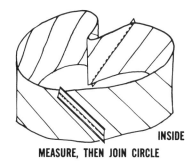

MEASURE, THEN JOIN CIRCLE

INSIDE

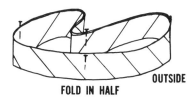

FOLD IN HALF

OUTSIDE

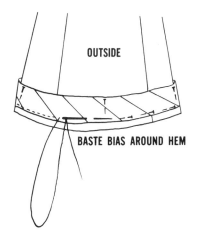

OUTSIDE

BASTE BIAS AROUND HEM

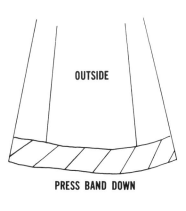

OUTSIDE

PRESS BAND DOWN

Figure 6-7. Lengthening Flared and Princess Dresses

cut edges downward. Pin, matching center-back and center-front to the half-way marks of the border—then match the side quarter marks. Ease on the border, patting it flat, and pin along the old hemline (or line you have marked, if the hem was uneven). Baste firmly. Put a few pins in the border above the bastings, to hold it straight while you stitch. Now sew your border ½″ above the cut edges. Pull out bastings, press border down flat. Trim inside edges evenly, and finish neatly, by pinking or overcasting. Press once more and it is ready to wear.

Making a Suspendered Skirt From An Old Dress
(Figure 6-8)

If a child has outgrown the bodice of a perfectly good dress, you can always cut off the top, make a belt of the bodice material, and buy a sweater to match the color of the dress, or one of the print colors. This is not hard to do—you simply cut the bodice about 2″ above the waist, turn fabric over inside into a band, and hem it over the waist seam. Hook the back to fasten and you have a skirt.

Sometimes you can combine two outgrown dresses to make one skirt.

To do this, cut off the top of one bodice and hem it over, forming a waistband. Cut strips from the second skirt, join them together, and use them to lengthen the skirt you have just sewn. You can make a waistband or suspenders out of material from the second skirt, and buy a little sweater or blouse to be worn with it, either in the color of the first skirt, or one that matches the border and suspenders. You can work out all kinds of variations on this idea.

CUT 2″ ABOVE WAIST

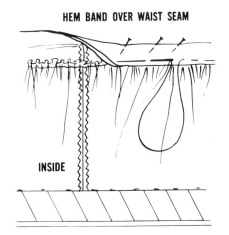

HEM BAND OVER WAIST SEAM

INSIDE

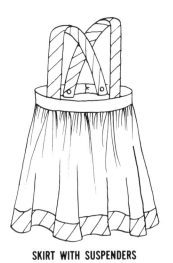

SKIRT WITH SUSPENDERS

Figure 6-8. Making a Suspendered Skirt from an Old Dress

7. Replacing Broken Zippers

How to Replace a Broken Zipper On a Skirt
(Figure 7-1)

To BEGIN with, clip the thread that holds the zipper and remove it. Never try to tear it out without first cutting the threads, as this will certainly stretch the fabric, and may even tear it. Brush off all threads. Where the zipper is sewn into the waistband at the top, remove fasteners, cut the thread at the waistband, and pull out the zipper tape.

Next, take the new zipper and place it under the back part of the skirt, teeth almost touching the fold of the skirt material. The pull-tab should be about 1/4" from the waistband. Tuck the zipper tape at the top inside the waistband, and pin down all along the fold of the seam until you reach the end of the zipper. Be careful not to stretch the skirt material. Stitch this by hand, using double thread in the needle (a No. 8 Crewel is good) and making your stitches about 1/4" long on the wrong side, 1/8" or less on the outside, and keeping them 1/8" away from the zipper teeth. You do not sew a zipper too close to the teeth because it would make the slide catch in the material when you pull the pull-tab up or down. When you reach the bottom, fasten off inside very firmly.

Pin the skirt placket closed over the zipper (working on the outside) with a line of pins holding the two folded edges of the placket opening together. Be sure the top front and back of the skirt meet exactly where it was stitched to the waistband. Pin the zipper down about 5/8" from the closed edge of the fold. Sew the zipper up the front side of the skirt opening along the pins, stitches 1/4" long on the inside (on the zipper tape) and 1/8" or less on the outside. When you reach the top, tuck the zipper tape inside the waistband and fasten off. Turn the skirt inside out, and stitch the tape ends at the bottom of the zipper to the skirt seam. This gives it extra firmness at the bottom.

Sew back the waistband, replacing it on the original stitching line, sewing the outside first, and then hemming back the inside. Replace the hooks and eyes. Press thoroughly with a steam iron, using a pressing cloth to protect silks or shiny fabrics. Press on the wrong side, unless it is a very thick tweed, which may need pressing on both sides. Be careful not to make a "shine" on the fabric. If you are using one of the newer nylon zippers, read the instructions in the package carefully. Nylon melts under high heat, so you may have to use a lukewarm iron or double pressing cloth. It is a good idea to press the whole skirt, especially the side that has been rezippered.

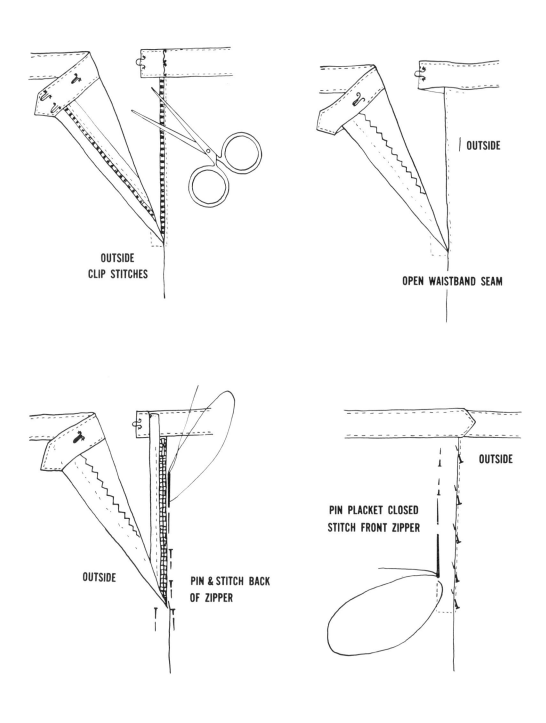

**OUTSIDE
CLIP STITCHES**

OUTSIDE

OPEN WAISTBAND SEAM

OUTSIDE

**PIN & STITCH BACK
OF ZIPPER**

**PIN PLACKET CLOSED
STITCH FRONT ZIPPER**

OUTSIDE

Figure 7-1. How to Replace a Broken Zipper On a Skirt

52

How to Replace a Broken Zipper On a Dress
(Figure 7-2)

For a center-back zipper that is set with one side right against the fabric, the other side with a deep fold of fabric entirely covering the zipper, you do it exactly the same way as you do a skirt, only you do not have to tuck the top tape into a waistband. Instead, turn it over and hem it to the inside of the neck of the dress and put your hook and eye on the top at the neck closing.

If the zipper you are removing is set in with an equal fold of material on either side, then your zipper must be centered. You do this by opening the zipper, and setting it under one side (it does not matter which side you do first), putting the teeth just underneath the fold so that they are completely covered. Using the old stitching line as a guide, sew down the side to the bottom, and fasten off securely. Then close the zipper, and pin down the other side so that the fold of the dress material meets the opposite side, covering the zipper completely. You can sew this side down with the zipper closed or open, whichever you find easier. Then turn the dress inside out, and sew the bottom zipper tape to the seam. Turn in the tape at the neckline neatly and hem it down, put back the hook and eye, and all you have to do is press it, and it is done. You do a center-back skirt seam exactly the same way, except that you tuck the top zipper tape inside the waistband, sew back the waistband, and put the hooks and eyes on the waistband just as you did at the side of the skirt.

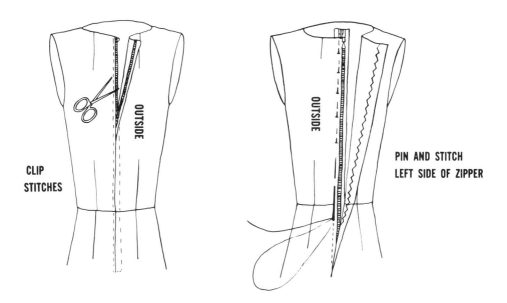

CLIP STITCHES

OUTSIDE

OUTSIDE

PIN AND STITCH LEFT SIDE OF ZIPPER

Figure 7-2. How to Replace a Broken Zipper On a Dress

53

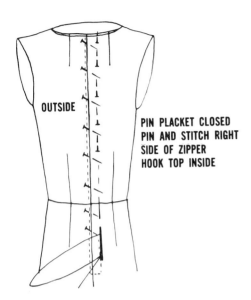

OUTSIDE

PIN PLACKET CLOSED
PIN AND STITCH RIGHT
SIDE OF ZIPPER
HOOK TOP INSIDE

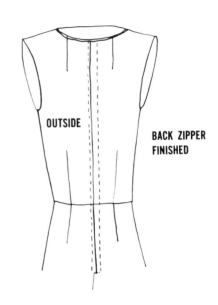

OUTSIDE

BACK ZIPPER
FINISHED

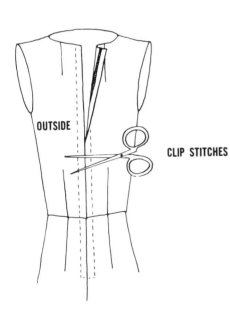

OUTSIDE

CLIP STITCHES

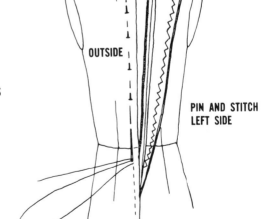

OUTSIDE

PIN AND STITCH
LEFT SIDE

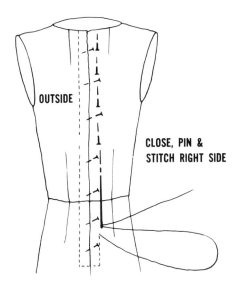
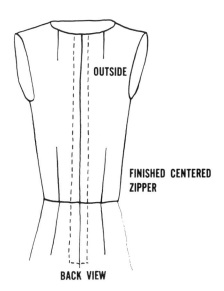

Figure 7-2. How to Replace a Broken Zipper On a Dress

How to Replace Side Underarm Zipper (Figure 7-3)

Many dresses have zippers set in at the left side from just below the sleeve seam to the hip line. These often break at the waistline where they get the most strain.

To replace a side underarm zipper, first look it over thoroughly and see how it is set in. Usually side zippers are done in one of two ways—the back of the dress close to the teeth and a wide front fold over the zipper to cover it; or, the back and front folds of the dress each half-way over the zipper.

First clip the stitches and brush off bits of thread and fuzz. If the old zipper was put in with the back of the dress close to the teeth, put your zipper in the same way, following the old stitching line. Be careful not to stretch the dress as you put it over the zipper. Pin it down the back side of the dress, and then sew it $\frac{1}{8}''$ away from the zipper teeth, with stitches $\frac{1}{4}''$ long on the wrong side (zipper tape side) and $\frac{1}{8}''$ long on the right (outside) side, using double thread. Fasten off securely at the bottom. Now lap the dress front over the zipper until the fold meets the dress back you have just sewn. If there is a waistline seam, be sure the front and back meet exactly at this seam. Pin the front fold to the zipper $\frac{5}{8}''$ from the closing. Stitch as before.

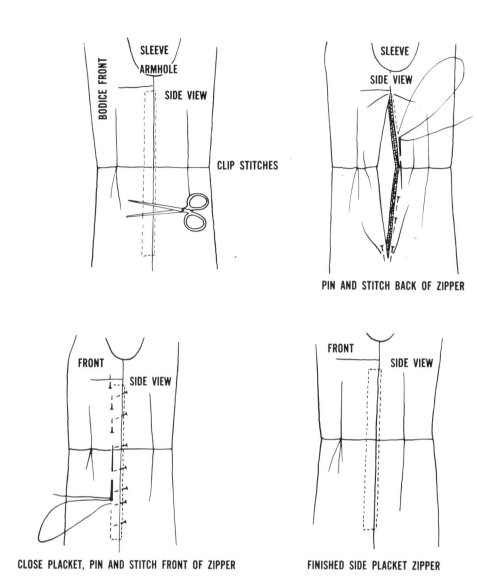

Figure 7-3. Replacing a Side Underarm Zipper

8. How to Make a Cummerbund and Scarf Set

FOR a cummerbund and scarf you will need a large square of material, preferably something rather soft, and not too bulky—jersey, taffeta, surah, silk crepe, challis, etc. Or you can use a very large handkerchief—one that is a yard and a quarter square or more.

If the material you choose is only 36″ wide, it will only make a small cummerbund (or sash) and very small triangle scarfs. These are fine for children, but for adults I recommend something larger.

If the material is:

36″ wide	. . . . .	buy 1 yard
39″ wide	. . . . .	buy 1⅛ yards
42-45″ wide	. . .	buy 1¼ yards
48-50″ wide	. .	buy 1⅜ yards
54″ wide	. . . . .	buy 1½ yards

When the sales clerk cuts your material from the bolt, be sure it is cut perfectly straight at *both* ends. You need a square, and it must be straight at all four sides. The important thing is that you buy a piece that is as long as it is wide.

Making a Cummerbund and Scarf Set (Figure 8-1)

Begin by pressing out any folds or creases; then lay the material flat on the table, right-side up. Fold it in half diagonally, right sides together, wrong side out. Pin along the fold, and be careful not to let the fabric twist or ripple. Pin along the edges.

Decide how wide you would like your cummerbund to be—anywhere from 4″ to about 8″. Do not make it too wide—it is going to be double thickness and crushed together. Mark a line parallel to the fold, ½″ wider than the width you have decided on. Cut through both layers. Pin the two edges together.

If you are making a winter scarf of wool jersey, then pin the two triangles together ½″ from the edges all around, and make your scarf double thickness. If you are doing a summer outfit, it is advisable to make the scarf single—then you will have *two* triangles, one to wear over your head, and one to go around your neck.

Stitch along the seam of the long bias piece, and stitch around the scarf (if it is double) making your seams ½″ wide. Leave a small opening (about 1½″) on one straight side of the triangular scarf, for turning it inside out. If you are making two single thickness scarves, turn the edges over ¼″ all around and stitch by machine. If you do not have a machine, then just press them over ¼″. Then turn the edge over again another ¼″, and hem all around. This looks much nicer if you do it by hand, of course, although machining

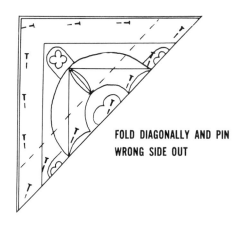

FOLD DIAGONALLY AND PIN
WRONG SIDE OUT

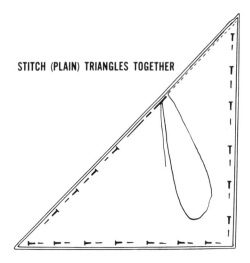

STITCH (PLAIN) TRIANGLES TOGETHER

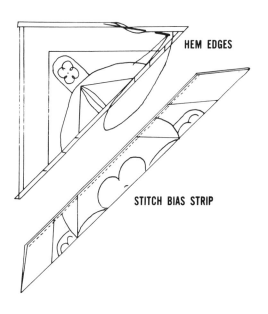

HEM EDGES

STITCH BIAS STRIP

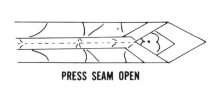

PRESS SEAM OPEN

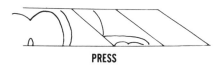

PRESS

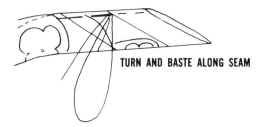

TURN AND BASTE ALONG SEAM

Figure 8-1. Making a Cummerbund
and Scarf Set

is alright if it is for very casual wear.

Now, press all along the seam of the cummerbund, opening it as you go, and being very careful not to press any creases in the other part of the material. This can be done easily on the side of the sleeve board. Press open the seams of the triangle, too, taking care not to press creases in the fabric.

Turn the sash and scarf right-side out. Now take your needle, and baste all along the seams, both sides folded back, so that the stitching is exactly on the edge, and the two sides look exactly alike and are evenly together. Do not let one edge roll over or show more on one side. Press flat with a thin cloth between the iron and the fabric. Also press the fold side very lightly. Press the scarf too.

Turn in the ends of the cummerbund, either square or pointed, whichever you prefer—baste and slip-stitch, then press. Slip-stitch the little opening in the side of the scarf, and press. You now have a very nice cummerbund and scarf ensemble.

A cummerbund is generally worn wound tightly around the waist and crushed into soft folds. The ends are tied in a knot on one side, or in the center back, or wherever you will. However if you prefer a single width around the waist, there is no reason why you should not wear it tied in a bow or a knot with long ends. The same goes for the neck or head scarf. Try tying it on one shoulder with a pin on the other shoulder to hold it in place, or sew a weight in the center of the bias side; then tie it loosely at the center back, forming a cowl in front. There are many ways to vary a scarf collar, and you will find it fun to experiment.

If you use a gay handkerchief square to make this set, you will have two matching triangle scarves (and only one side to hem on each) and a sash with fancy ends all ready hemmed. This is a very smart and attractive way to dress up a plain linen or silk dress—you will have a matching scarf, sash, and head-kerchief. Or you can make a two-piece ensemble in black satin to liven up a black wool dress. Use a bright color contrast to brighten up a dull dress. There are many ideas, and you will often get inspirations from just looking at lovely fabrics in the stores.

9. How to Make a Dirndl Skirt

A DIRNDL skirt is a gathered, full skirt of straight-grain fabric, sewn onto a waistband. It is about the easiest kind of skirt you can make.

There are many pretty materials on the market nowadays that are specially printed for making dirndl skirts. In almost any yard goods store that carries moderately large selections, you will find several pieces that are printed with decorative borders, or a design that runs lengthway along the fabric parallel to one selvage, the other selvage side plain. If you choose one of these, you simply buy 2 to 4 yards, depending on how full you wish to make your skirt. And remember to buy a matching skirt zipper, some 1″ wide belting, thread and hooks.

Making a Bordered Dirndl Skirt (Figure 9-1)

You begin by tearing or cutting the two ends of your material so that they are quite straight. Fold the material in half, right sides together, cut ends together, and make a seam along the cut side ⅝″ wide. Press the seam open.

Now turn up the hem. You must decide how close to the edge you wish the design to come, and turn the hem up accordingly. If you are uncertain, make your hem 2½″ or 3″ wide—it is always safe. You will probably find that the selvage will serve for the top edge of the hem, and it will need no seam-binding or turning in, unless the selvage drags or is too tight. In that case, you must cut it off and put seam-binding on the edge. Pin the hem up evenly all around, and slip-stitch it so that it does not show on the right side. Press smoothly. If there is a crease along the center of the material, press that out also.

Measure the length you wish the skirt to be from waist to hem. It is better to measure a skirt you already have and know to be the correct length, than to try and measure yourself. Measure the length in the center-front and center-back from the waist seam to the hem-edge.

Now, fold the material in half crosswise, right side of the fabric inside, with the seam for the center-back, the fold for the center-front. Lay it flat on the table (in half). Pin the hem edges together accurately. Mark the center-front fold with contrasting thread, then mark a point half-way between the back seam and the center-front fold, on both layers. This is for the sides.

Next, starting from the hem, measure the length of the center front along the fold, upward from the hem, and mark this point with a pin or chalk. Then measure the length of the center-back along the seam, upward from the hem, and mark this point also. Make a straight line from the center-front mark to the center-back mark.

If you are lucky enough to have a waistline that is perfectly straight then your skirt, front and back, will

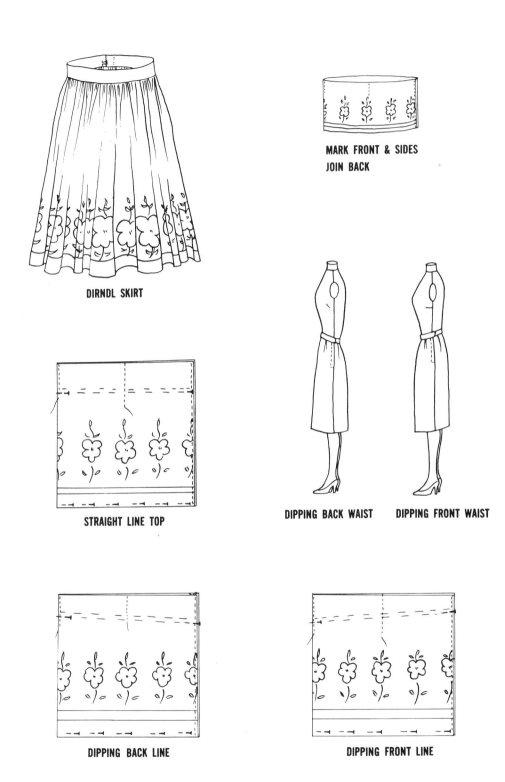

DIRNDL SKIRT

MARK FRONT & SIDES
JOIN BACK

STRAIGHT LINE TOP

DIPPING BACK WAIST   DIPPING FRONT WAIST

DIPPING BACK LINE

DIPPING FRONT LINE

Figure 9-1. Making a Bordered Dirndl Skirt

measure about the same, and the top line you have just drawn will be straight along the fabric.

If your waistline dips down in the back, the skirt front will be a little longer than the back; the back about 1″ to 1½″ shorter, so the top line will run very slightly down toward the back seam.

If your hips tend to be rather large in back or your front waistline dips, then your skirt will measure a little longer in back than in front, and the top line will tilt upward very slightly toward the back seam.

When you have your top line marked, make another line of marks ⅝″ above it. This is for seam-allowance. Cut along this line. Open the back seam, 8″ down, and put the zipper in as previously directed, with the top of the zipper about 1″ from the cut edge of the waistline.

Now you put in two rows of gatherings, one row ⅝″ from the edge, one row ⅜″ from the edge. If you do it by machine, you put the stitch regulator to the largest size stitch, loosen the tension slightly, and machine around from zipper-top to zipper-top.

Hand-gathering (Figure 9-2)

If you do it by hand, this is how to put in hand-gatherings: You are going to pull up two (or more) yards of material on two rows of thread until it is the right size for your waist. Therefore you need to use either an extra strong thread, such as nylon (nylast, heavy-duty), or else your regular thread *doubled*. Thread your needle with thread considerably longer than your waist measurement.

RUNNING STITCH

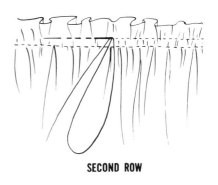

SECOND ROW

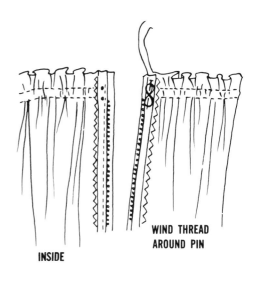

INSIDE

WIND THREAD AROUND PIN

Figure 9-2. Hand-gathering

Hand-gathering is done with a stitch called a "running-stitch." It is quick and easy. You start with a *big* knot, $\frac{5}{8}''$ from the top edge of the material. Then holding the needle and fabric between the right-hand thumb and first finger (reverse this if you are left-handed), and pushing the needle with the thimble on the middle finger, sew with small stitches toward the left hand, which holds the material taut. The needle point just about touches the left index finger as it runs forward with each tiny stitch. You do several stitches at a time, and pull the thread through now and then, pushing the fabric along the thread as it is gathered up. When you have put the first row of running stitches all around, do *not* fasten off but cut the thread, and pull the needle off, knot the thread end, and leave it dangling. Then rethread your needle, and put in the second row $\frac{1}{4}''$ above the first row.

Now take the two dangling ends of thread, and pull them up until they are even, and push the fabric along the threads until it measures $\frac{1}{2}''$ more than your waist measurement. Put a pin in between the thread ends, and wind them around it to hold the gathers, but do not fasten off or cut the threads yet. Lay this aside.

Doing the Waistband
(Figure 9-3)

Next comes the waistband. Cut a strip $2\frac{1}{2}''$ wide along the top selvage, and cut it $3\frac{1}{2}''$ larger than your waist measurement. Remember—you may want to tuck in a blouse or sweater, so do not make it too tight. Fold this band in half crosswise, and

then pin the cut ends together $1\frac{1}{2}''$ from the edges. (The ends are for a point and extension where it fastens, so do not cut them off). Mark the half-way and quarter distances along the band for the center-front and sides.

Put the waistband over the skirt, so that the upper cut edges are together, and right sides of the fabric come together, with the pinned part of the band at the zipper top, and the center-front band at the center-front of the skirt. Then match the side marks. Pin the skirt to the band all around, keeping the gathered fullness even, and pinning in between the two rows of gathering stitches. Baste and try on, just to make sure it is right. (It *should* fit nicely, if you measured accurately.)

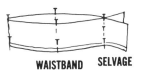

WAISTBAND   SELVAGE

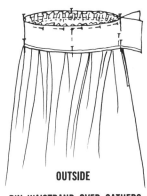

OUTSIDE

PIN WAISTBAND OVER GATHERS

Figure 9-3. Doing the Waistband

64

But if you have to make the waistband a bit tighter, you can just push the gathering back a little on each side of the zipper. If you have to let it out a bit, then pull the gathering a little looser. (That is why you did not finish off the gathering thread, or sew up the waistband—you can pull out the pin and ease the gathers, and you have enough on the ends of the band to let it out easily.) When the waistline is adjusted to your satisfaction, sew the skirt to the waistband through the gatherings, between the two rows of stitches. Be careful not to let the gathers bunch up, or the band fold under the presser foot if you are machining it. If you are sewing it by hand, then it is a good idea to put two rows of stitches along the waist seam. When this seam is stitched, pull out the bastings, and press the waistband upward.

Putting on the Belt (Figure 9-4)

Now take your belting, and baste it along the inside of the waistband, the lower edge of the belting just touching the stitches of the seam. Then turn in the end of the left side, turn the waistband over the belting to meet the stitching line, and hem very neatly, so that the gatherings and belting are covered. You will find that the edge of the selvage just meets the stitching line so you will not need to turn anything in. The selvage makes a nice flat finish. When you reach the top end (that is, the right-hand side), fold the belting over to make a point that starts at the edge of the zipper fold. Trim off any spare belting and fabric, fold

the fabric over the point, and hem neatly. Press it very flat all around—especially at the point and end.

Sew on two No. 2 hooks at the base of the point, and put the bars on the opposite side of the waistband. Put another hook and bar at the end of the extension. You also might make two hang-up loops of seambinding or narrow ribbon, and sew them on the inside of the waistband on each side. Now it is ready for you to wear.

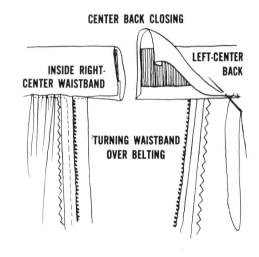

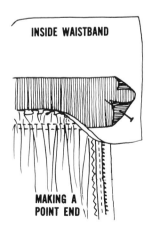

Figure 9-4. Putting On the Belting

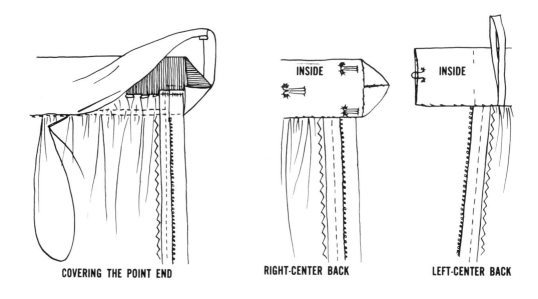

COVERING THE POINT END

RIGHT-CENTER BACK

LEFT-CENTER BACK

SIDE FASTENING

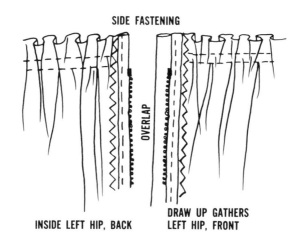

OVERLAP

INSIDE LEFT HIP, BACK

DRAW UP GATHERS LEFT HIP, FRONT

10. How to Make a Circular Skirt Without a Pattern

Women's Circular Skirts

BEFORE you buy the material, you must know how much to buy. You start by only taking two measurements. First measure your waistline, and second, measure the length of your favorite skirt from the waistline to the hem. Add two or three inches to the skirt length measurement and multiply this by four. Add this to your waist measurement. This is the amount you will need to buy.

For skirts in sizes up to 30" waist and 28" length, material 36" to 42" wide is best. Wider material is alright, but it is very difficult to fold, and there is much waste—so you will do well to keep to a 42" width (or less) for your first effort.

For example, let us suppose your waist measures 24" and your skirt is 21" long. Add 3" to the skirt length (for hem-allowance): 21 plus 3 equals 24, multiply this by 4 and you have 96; add the waist measurement (96 plus 24) and you have 120". This is 3⅜ yards (dividing inches by 36 to get yards, to the nearest ⅛ yard). If you are taller, or your waist measures more, or if you want a longer skirt, you will need a little more, and if you are shorter or your waist is smaller, you will need a little less.

Choose a plain material, or one that does not have any stripes or pattern which must go in one direction. A circular skirt falls in every direc-

tion, so a one-way print does not work out well. Tiny checks, irregular polka dots, or all-over prints are fine. So are plain cottons, woolens, dacron, acetate, arnel, etc. If this is your first try at making something, it is best to use a fairly firm cotton—such as gingham—for a beginning. It is inexpensive, pretty and not difficult to handle.

When you have bought your material, remember to get a skirt zipper (7" or 8", open top) about a yard of belting (the rayon and cotton kind, medium stiff, is good), a spool of thread to match, and a 7-yard roll of seam-binding (unless you intend to overcast the hem-edge). Also hooks and eyes, size 2, and plenty of silk pins (No. 17) are necessary.

Folding and Pinning the Circular Skirt (Figure 10-1)

Now if the material is creased or pulled crooked, press it out flat and straight. This will make the material easier to fold, and your skirt will hang better because it is cut evenly.

Then lay it flat on the table, and fold it in half along the width, right sides together, cut ends and selvages together. Smooth it down nicely. Fold it in half again across the width, selvages together; the first fold now comes on the cut ends. This gives you a rectangle four layers thick. Put a few pins in here and there, to hold it together smoothly.

Place one finger on the top corner of the double folds, and with the other hand take the bottom corner of the double folds and fold the material diagonally across until the folds meet the selvages, and you have a large triangle eight layers thick. Check carefully to be sure the selvages and folds are together, and smooth.

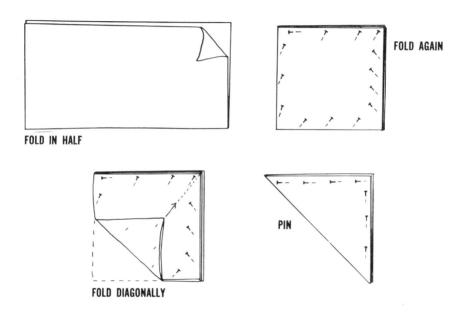

Figure 10-1. Folding and Pinning Circular Skirt

Preparing The Waistline
(Figure 10-2)

Now we mark the waistline. To do this, find your own waist measurement in this list of sizes.

If your waist measures:

21½, 22, 22½ inches ...... mark a line 3½ inches down.
23, 23½, 24 inches .... mark a line 3¾ inches down.
24½, 25, 25½ inches ...... mark a line 4 inches down.
26, 26½, 27 inches .... mark a line 4¼ inches down.
27½, 28, 29 inches .... mark a line 4½ inches down.
30, 31, 31½ inches .... mark a line 4¾ inches down.
32, 32½, 33 inches .... mark a line 5 inches down.

With your ruler, measure down the selected distance from the folded point at the top of the triangle and mark, with pins or chalk, a fan-shaped curved line for your waist. Then mark a line 5/8" *above* this curved line (that is, nearer the point) for the seam-allowance.

Cut carefully along the top line of the marks. If it is too hard to cut through all eight layers of the material at once, cut two or four layers at a time, making sure you cut each layer along the same line, so that they are all even when you finish.

From the line that marks the waistline (that is, 5/8" below the cut) measure your skirt length, *plus* 2" or 3" for hem-allowance, and put another line of marks fan-wise across the lower (or near center, depending on your skirt length) part of the triangle. Be sure to keep your tape measure or yardstick moving fan-wise. Do not make all the marks from the same place, but move the top of the measure along the cut curve slightly, measuring from the line of waistline marks, spreading out the marks at the bottom. When you have marked this line, check to see that it is a good curve, then cut carefully, as you did at the top. Here again, you may find it easier to cut two or four layers at a time, but be sure they all end up on the same curve. You now have two half-circles, with a small half-circle for the waistline cut out of the selvage side.

Lay one on top of the other, right sides of the material facing, selvages together. Pin about 5/8" from the edge. Stitch all the way down one side from top (small circle) to bottom, taking a 5/8" seam. Stitch the other side the same way, only starting 8" from the small circle. Baste

this seam. This is where you put in the zipper. Press both seams open and flat. They probably will not need any edge finishing, as they are selvages. However sometimes selvages have a tendency to pull up, or drag, and if they do this, then you can either nick them in about 1/8" every few inches, or else pink off the very edge.

Now turn your skirt right-side out, pull the bastings out of the top-side seam. Put the zipper in as instructed on page 51, starting 1" from the top edge with the back seam fold against the teeth, and the front seam fold lapped over to cover the zipper. This is for a left hip closing.

From the leftover material, you cut a strip 3" wide and 3" longer than your waist measurement. You will have pieces left over. Cut your waistband along the selvage of the material, making a diagonal join if you cannot get it all out of the center (or large) triangle. Press open the join, and put it at the side of the skirt above the side seam. (If you have to make a join, both pieces should be the same length—half your waist measure, plus 2". Be sure to cut it long enough—it is a good idea to join the two pieces before cutting the length.)

Fold the waistband in half across the width, and pin it together 1½" from the ends. The ends are left for making a point on top, and an underside extension where it fastens. Mark the half and quarters.

Next, put the waistband over the top of the skirt, right sides of fabric together, top edges of the skirt and band together. Pin the pinned side of the waistband to the zipper side of the skirt, the half-way mark to the opposite side seam, and the

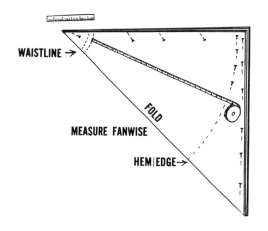

WAISTLINE →

FOLD

MEASURE FANWISE

HEM|EDGE →

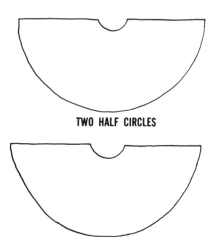

TWO HALF CIRCLES

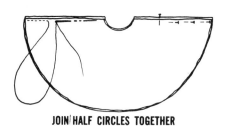

JOIN|HALF CIRCLES TOGETHER

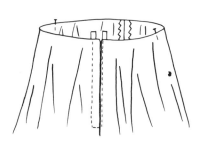

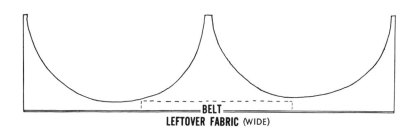

BELT

LEFTOVER FABRIC (WIDE)

70

BELT
LEFTOVER FABRIC (NARROW)

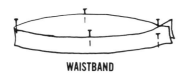

WAISTBAND

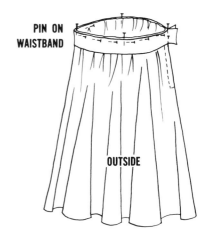

PIN ON WAISTBAND

OUTSIDE

Figure 10-2. Marking the Waistline

quarter marks of the band to the center-front and center-back of the skirt. Then pin the skirt and band together all the way around ½″ from the edges. If the skirt is a little tight for the band, nick the top edge along the curve, making the nicks not more than ⅛″ deep. If it is a little looser than the band, ease in some fullness —it will ease without puckering at the sides where the curve cuts across the bias. Keep the center-front and center-back smooth.

Baste this seam, unpin the side, and try it on. Do not make your waistband too tight—remember it will feel tighter when the belting is inside and the band hemmed over. And remember too, you will probably want to tuck a blouse inside, or maybe a sweater. So go easy on the tightness.

If you do have to make it tighter or looser, you must re-mark your half and quarter distances on the waistband, and move the skirt center-front and center-back and sides to the new marks. Then even out the skirt fullness, keeping the center-front and center-back smooth.

Putting in the Belting
(Figure 10-3)

When you have the waistline comfortably fitted, machine or hand stitch the waist seam along the basted line, pull out the bastings, and press the waistband upward. Now take your belting, and pin it around the waistband with the lower edge touching the line you have just stitched, inside the fold. You can pin or baste this, but it is easier to handle if you baste it. Then starting an inch or so from the zipper, fold the waistband tightly over the belting, turn in the lower edge (you allowed ½" for this) and hem it to the stitching line. Then turn the top-front end of the belting and band over to form a point and hem the ends in neatly. Turn in the edge of the back belting and band, leaving an extension about 1"

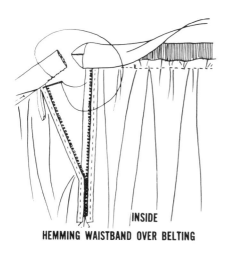

HEMMING WAISTBAND OVER BELTING

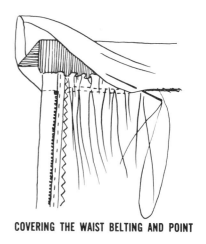

COVERING THE WAIST BELTING AND POINT

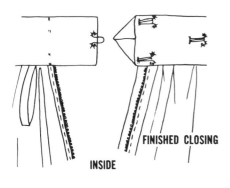

INSIDE   **FINISHED CLOSING**

FINISHED SKIRT

Figure 10-3. Putting in the Belting

or 1¼" for smooth fastening. Press very flat and sew on two hooks (size 2) just inside the point, and one at the end of the extension.

Now you must be eager to finish the skirt and wear it, but this is where a little patience pays off. You will find that most fabrics sag where they hang on the bias. To save having to do your hem over again, it is best to clip your skirt onto a hanger, and let it hang for a day or two. If possible, let it hang by an open window, or in the bathroom, where slightly damp air can blow on it. This will help it to fall softly and set the folds gracefully.

When it seems to have finished sagging, put it on, mark the hemline, and hem it as directed in Chapter 5. When you give it its final pressing, be careful to press it up-and-down, not side-to-side. Do not press out the bias part where it has sagged, or you will make your hem uneven; after all, you waited a couple of days for it to drop—so do not undo it with the iron!

If you hang your skirts on hangers, you might sew a couple of loops of seam-binding inside the waistband, one at each side. But a circular skirt keeps its shape better if you use a clip-hanger, and clip it on so that the waistband is held straight. Now the skirt is finished.

Children's Circular Skirts

Circular skirts can be made for children of all ages and held up by suspenders made from strips of left-over material. You need considerably less material for children's skirts, however, as they are much shorter and you can often make a child's skirt without any side seams at all.

Folding the Material for Children's Skirts (Figure 10-4)

For instance, a child's skirt that is going to be 10" long, with a 1½" hem and, say, a 20" waist, will measure 33" to 34" across from side-hem-across-waist-to-side-hem, and so it can be cut from 1 yard of 36" material—one whole circle. You follow the same procedure for larger skirts, only fold the material *lengthwise* first, then in half crosswise (once only), then diagonally—just like folding a handkerchief. When it is cut, it looks like a very large dough-nut.

Putting In the Zipper (Figure 10-5)

For the zipper, you make a side slash and face it. Mark a line, with thread, on the crosswise grain of the fabric, probably about 5" down from the center hole (the size depends on how large the skirt is and how deep you want the zipper opening to be). Baste a strip of fabric 3" wide and 1" longer than the opening over this mark, on the left side of the skirt, right sides of the material together.

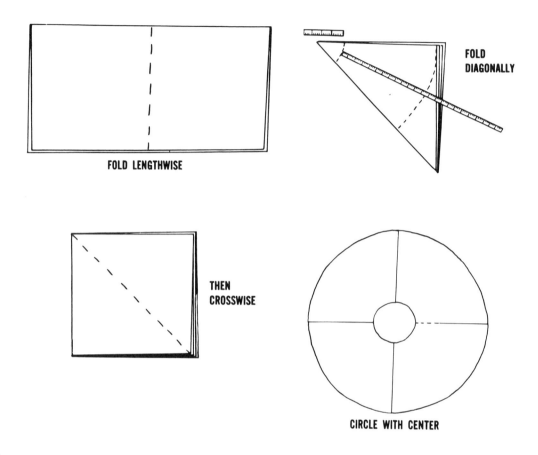

Figure 10-4. Folding Material for Children's Skirt

(If you want the zipper in the center-back instead, then you make your thread mark on the straight grain of the fabric instead of crosswise.) Stitch with small stitches about ⅛″ on each side of the thread line, making a neat square at the bottom end. It is advisable to stitch this twice. Cut carefully along the thread mark in between the stitching lines, clip-ping the bottom tiny square end in an upside-down Y. Turn the facing inside the skirt, pressing it so that the facing does not show outside.

Then put in the zipper, the top of the zipper starting an inch below the top of the opening. Set on the waistband, let it hang, and then finish the hem just as you did for the larger size.

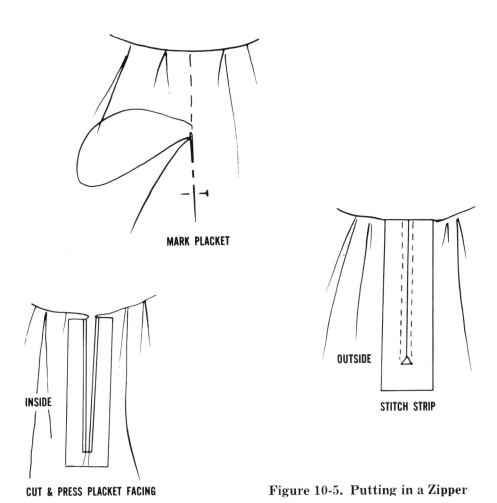

MARK PLACKET

CUT & PRESS PLACKET FACING

INSIDE

OUTSIDE

STITCH STRIP

Figure 10-5. Putting in a Zipper

Making Suspenders
(Figure 10-6)

You can make suspenders by joining 3″ wide strips of leftover material, folding them in half lengthwise and stitching along the sides with ½″ seam. Turn inside out (with a large pin or a turning hook), press and sew onto the skirt in front inside the waistband. You divide the front width of the waistband by three, and set each suspender on at the one-third mark. Put the skirt on the child, pull the suspenders over the shoulders and cross them over in back, pin at the desired height to the back waistband. Take it off, and sew the suspenders firmly. Or put hooks or snap fasteners on the ends. If you prefer buttons and buttonholes, it is advisable that you either make the button holes by machine or go to a shop that does buttonholes, pleating and picoting. Much work is required to put a bound buttonhole in the end of a suspender strap after you have once finished it.

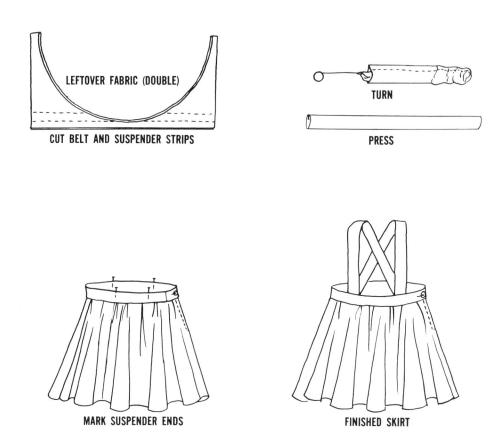

LEFTOVER FABRIC (DOUBLE)

CUT BELT AND SUSPENDER STRIPS

TURN

PRESS

MARK SUSPENDER ENDS

FINISHED SKIRT

Figure 10-6. Making Suspenders

11. Two Ways to Make Buttonholes

Bias Bound Buttonholes (Figure 11-1)

MARK the place and size where the buttonhole is to be with thread stitches. Then cut a strip of *bias* material 1½″ longer than the buttonhole length, and 2″ wide, and crease it lengthwise along the center. Lay this strip over the stitches line, the center crease on the stitches, right sides of the fabric facing each other. Pin or baste around the edge. Now sew around the line of the buttonhole, making your stitches ⅛″ from the line, and turning at right angles when you reach the ends, with 3 or 4 stitches at each end across the width. Count your stitches as you sew, making the same number on each side, and the same number at each end. When stitching around a buttonhole, the stitching should be done from the garment side, where the tracing line is, rather than from the patch side. This is how it is done with a sewing machine. If you do it by hand, you must use extremely small stitches, rather tight, and sew twice around the same place. With the little embroidery scissors, cut the buttonhole along the first line of marking stitches in the exact center, clipping into the corners in a Y-shaped nick.

Be *very* careful at these corners—the good shape of your buttonholes depends on keeping them very square and even. And be *extra* careful not to cut through the stitches, or you will be in trouble. It pays to take time and get it right.

Now turn the strip through the buttonhole and pull the ends gently. Flatten the corners with your thumbnail. If you are very good at using your iron daintily, you may be able to press the tiny side-seams open. If not, press them into the hole if the material is thin, or back into the garment if it is thick. From the outside, fold the strip material into a binding ⅛″ wide on each side of the buttonhole, and baste, keeping both sides perfectly even. Press. Stitch the tiny box-pleats at each end. Now press the back or facing into its proper position, and with the tips of your little scissors, cut the facing through the center of the buttonhole a *very* tiny bit longer than the buttonhole. Turn in the cut edges with the tip of your needle, and hem it around with very small stitches. Remove all bastings and press.

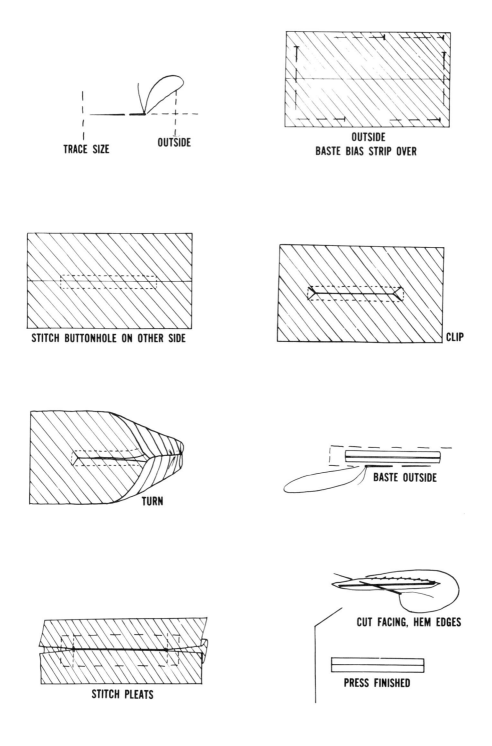

Figure 11-1. Bias Bound Buttonholes

Straight Bound Buttonholes (Figure 11-2)

Mark your buttonhole size and place with thread as before. Now cut a strip of material 1½" longer than the buttonhole, and 1" wide. Fold in half lengthwise, right side out, and press. Open it out flat, wrong side up, and fold the two cut edges over to the center crease so that they meet. Press.

Place this strip over the buttonhole stitches with the cut edges up, the center crease on the buttonhole stitches. With your machine, or with very tiny hand stitches, stitch around the buttonhole line ⅛" on each side of the center, making very square corners at each end. Overlap the stitches where they meet. Pull out the bastings and cut through the center very carefully, making a Y-shaped slash at each end. Turn the strip through the hole to the other side, pull the ends taut and press with your thumbnail. On the inside, stitch across the ends, so that the tiny folds are held in place. Press. Press back the facing, cut through the buttonhole, and hem as before.

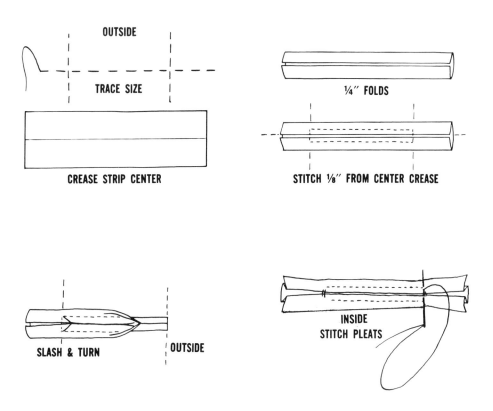

Figure 11-2. Straight Bound Buttonholes

12. How to Refit a Tailored Skirt

THERE are a number of ways to refit a tailored skirt, none of them particularly difficult, provided you are willing to give the work sufficient time and care. However you cannot do this kind of alteration in half an hour; it takes at least an afternoon to pin-fit, trace, rip, baste, try on, adjust, stitch and press the skirt.

The refitting alterations described here fall into the following categories:

1. A skirt that is too loose all over.

2. A skirt that fits at the top, but not down the sides.

3. A skirt that fits from the hips down, but is too loose around the top and waistline.

4. A skirt that cups in under the seat back.

5. A skirt that droops down in the front.

A Skirt that is Loose All Over (Figure 12-1)

Put your skirt on, remembering to wear the correct girdle and shoes, and fasten it up "as is." Make sure that it hangs straight. Pinch a fold in the waistband at the top of each side-seam until it fits comfortably around the waist, and pin these folds. It probably will be bulky and the pins may bend, but you must persevere as this is your new waist measurement.

Starting from the waistband pinches, pinch out a fold along the seam down each side, keeping the line of pins very straight and slanting out slightly toward the hem. Pin the zipper side as well, and be sure both sides are even. Do not fit your skirt too tightly, or it will pucker. It is alright to make it quite smooth and slick above the hipline, but below that, go easy. Remember you will want to walk and sit. So allow about 1½" to 2" of ease for movement from the hipline to the hem. A skirt that is fitted to the figure with no allowance for movement will cup in under the seat as the wearer walks. A well-fitted skirt should never be too tight.

When it is pinned to your satisfaction, mark the fitting lines around the zipper with pins or chalk, then open it and take off your skirt. Lay it flat on the table, right-side out. With contrasting colored thread, trace the alterations exactly where you have pinned them, on the outside of your skirt. Mark the waistband changes with separate thread because you are going to take it off. To trace, you make long stitches along the pinned lines, picking up only a thread or two of fabric, and being careful not to sew through and catch the material underneath. When you have done this on all the alterations, back and front and waistband, take out

TOO LOOSE
ALL THE WAY

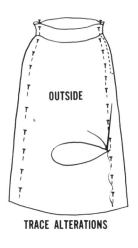

TRACE ALTERATIONS

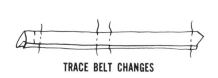

TRACE BELT CHANGES

PIN & BASTE ALTERATIONS

SIDES TRACED   CLIP STITCHES

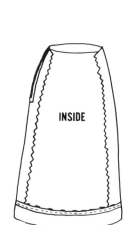

PRESS SEAMS OPEN

Figure 12-1. A Skirt that is
Too Loose All Over

the pins, and you will see your alterations nicely outlined in colored thread.

With your small scissors, clip the threads along the waistband and take it off. Clip the threads around the zipper and take it out. Undo the hem at each side seam for a few inches. Baste along the tracing lines, through *one* thickness of material so that the alteration lines show through on the inside of the skirt. Turn the skirt inside out and lay it flat on the table. Pin down the sides along the tracing lines, pinning the front and back together. From the hip, the line should slant slightly inward up to the waist, and slightly outward down toward the hem. There should be no bumps, lumps or curves. It helps a great deal to use a yardstick and piece of chalk to rule down these seams.

These side seams call for good judgment on your part. For a very straight skirt, these side seams should run at right angles to the hem up to the hipline (never inward from the hip down). If you walk with a long stride or tend to be heavy at the hips, the side seams should slant slightly outward from the hipline, to allow a little more ease in walking and sitting. However, whether your skirt is to be straight or eased, each side seam must be a straight line from hip to hem. And carry the side seams right on through the opened hem to the edge of the skirt.

When you have the seams pinned satisfactorily, baste them down with rather small stitches. With your small scissors, clip the thread along the old seam lines and undo the seams. Then press them open. Clip the top of the left side basting, and baste in the zipper. Set this aside.

Refitting the Waistband
(Figure 12-2)

Measure the amount you have traced on each side of the waistband for tightening. You will have one fairly large bit on the right-hand side, and a small bit on each side of waistband opening. Add these together and mark a point this distance from the old back-fastening line. Put the waistband around your waist and pin it closed at this new point to see if it fits comfortably. Do not make it too tight. There are two things to keep in mind: (1) Your skirt has to be sewn back inside the waistband, which will make it slightly tighter; and (2) You may want to wear a sweater or blouse tucked inside. So, again, go easy on the fitting.

Next open the waistband seam-allowance, and with the right sides of the material together, pin the front of the waistband opening to the top-front of the zipper, and the back of the waistband to the top-back of the zipper with the edge of the back zipper coming to the new closing mark you just made on the waistband. Pin the skirt to the waistband all around, following the old stitching lines, and keeping them evenly together. If the skirt is a little fuller than the waistband, ease the fullness in over the front hip bones and over the back hips, keeping it very even. Baste and try on.

When you are satisfied with the fit, stitch your skirt side seams and waistband. This should be done by machine if possible. If not, use a very small running stitch by hand, and sew twice along the same line exactly, keeping the stitches *very* straight. Put the zipper in by hand

MARK WAISTBAND SIZE

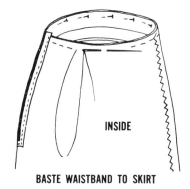
INSIDE

BASTE WAISTBAND TO SKIRT

Figure 12-2. Refitting the Waistband

(See Chapter 7). Remove all basting. Press the side seams open, the waistband seam up and the hem sides flat.

Hem the waistband over the seam inside the waistline, and sew on the hooks and eyes.

A Skirt that Fits at the Top, But Not Down the Sides
(Figure 12-3)

Put your skirt on and smooth it down over the hips. Then pinch in a fold down the side seams, starting from wherever the looseness begins and pin down the sides, slanting outward very slightly, right through the hem. If the zipper is too thick to pin double, you must make a tiny pleat in the skirt on each side of the zipper stitches (half the "take-in" amount on each side).

Having pinned the sides, take off the skirt. Trace, pin, baste, press and try on as before. Be careful not to let the side seams run inward across the grain of the fabric, as that often pulls the skirt into an ugly line and makes the top tend to bulge. Take out only the amount of material that is absolutely necessary. Try on, and when the fitting is satisfactory, sew up the seams, replace the zipper, stitch the hem sides, press and it is done.

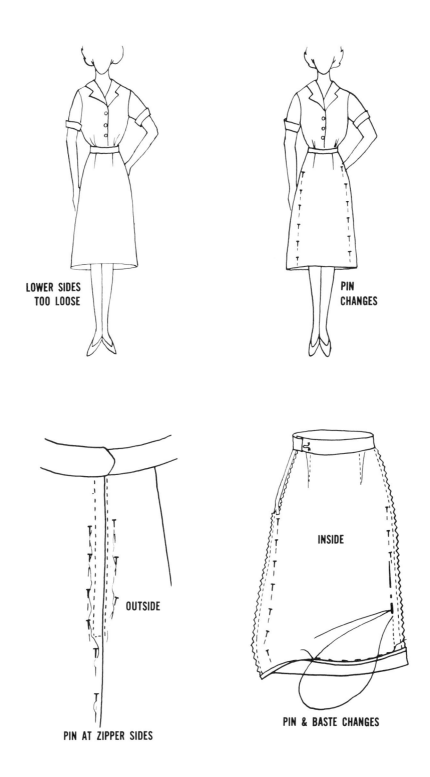

LOWER SIDES
TOO LOOSE

PIN
CHANGES

OUTSIDE

PIN AT ZIPPER SIDES

INSIDE

PIN & BASTE CHANGES

Figure 12-3. A Skirt that Fits at the Top, But Not Down the Sides

A Skirt that Fits from the Hips Down (Figure 12-4)

To do this alteration, you pin your alterations only to the hipline (or wherever it starts fitting correctly), instead of all the way down to the hem. Again wearing the proper undergarments and shoes, put your skirt on and smooth it down until it fits properly at the hips and lower part. Then pinch in a fold, or pleat, on the waistband at each side until it fits comfortably. Be sure you take out the same amount on each side. Then pin out a fold along the right-hand seam from the waistband to the hip, or wherever the skirt fits correctly, tapering out this fold to nothing at the bottom. On the left-hand side, pin out a small pleat on each side of the zipper, and lap the waistband over.

Then take off your skirt, and proceed as before—trace, pin, baste, rip, press and try it on. This alteration is the same as the first one—refitting the entire skirt—except that you do not have to do the lower part of the side seam or hem sides. And you may not have to take out the whole zipper —that will depend on how far down the alteration has to go.

This alteration takes more time because it is fussy, but it is quite an expensive alteration to have done by a tailor, so it is worthwhile spending an evening trying it.

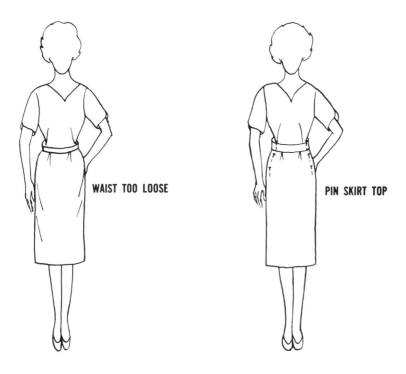

WAIST TOO LOOSE

PIN SKIRT TOP

Figure 12-4. A Skirt that Fits from the Hips Down

TRACE AND SEPARATE

INSIDE

A Skirt that Cups in Under the Seat Back
(Figure 12-5)

Many women have waistlines that dip down in the back. This is especially true of tall, slim, long-waisted girls. Often a ready-to-wear skirt will droop and hang inward at the back, or cup in under the seat. This fault cannot be corrected by tightening the skirt at the sides; instead the skirt must be raised across the back at the waistline seam.

To do this, first put on your skirt and smooth it down, with the side seams as straight as possible. Stand sideways in front of a long mirror. Standing perfectly straight, pinch up a fold in the center-back of the skirt as close to the waistband as possible. Pinch the fold up until the back hem is the same length as the front hem, and the center-back of the skirt hangs perfectly straight from hip to hem. From this center pinch, continue the fold across the back waistline both ways, tapering it out to nothing at the side seams. There will

be little wrinkles and puckers underneath the pins, but do not worry about that.

When you have adjusted the fold so that the back of the skirt hangs perfectly straight and the waistband sits comfortably at the natural waistline, take off the skirt and lay it on the table with the top toward you. With colored thread, trace both sides of the fold you have just pinched and pinned up. When you take out the pins, you will see your alteration is shaped something like an orange slice, with the lower curved line larger than the top.

Clip the waistband stitches across the back from side seam to zipper (do not touch the zipper) and separate it from the skirt.

Because you are curving the waistline further down, the new line is longer than the waistband. To make it fit on the waistband again, you must make the hip darts a little big-

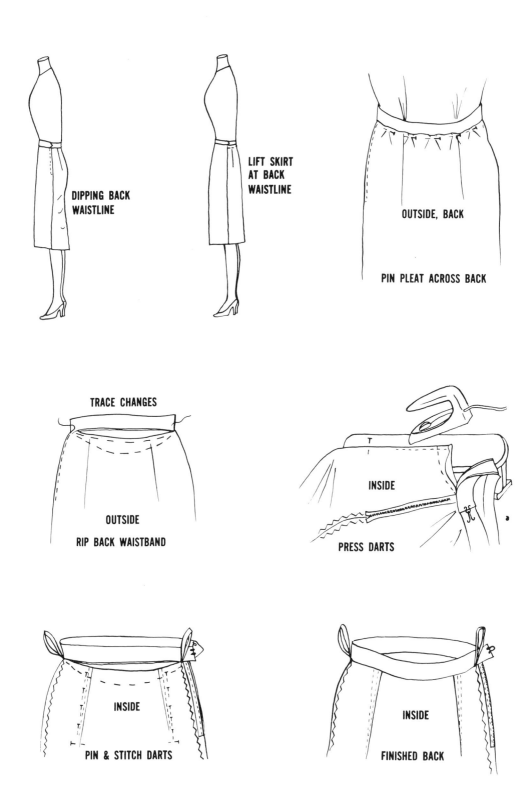

Figure 12-5. A Skirt that Cups Under the Seat Back

ger. They must also be slightly longer, as you are shortening them at the top.

Measure the waistband from side-seam to side-seam. Then measure the new curved line from side-seam to side-seam. Subtract the waistband measurement from the curved-line measurement and divide the result by four. This is the extra amount you must enlarge the hip-darts (double) at the place where the new curved line crosses them.

Turn the skirt inside out, and pin the hip darts down. As you are lowering the waistline, you must lengthen the darts the same amount. The easiest way to do this is to press them flat, away from the skirt, continuing the fold straight down about 1″ to 1½″ below the old stitching point. Measure the old dart from waist-seam to point. Make the new dart the same length, measuring from the new curved line down the fold you just pressed. (And remember to add the extra ¼-measurement

at the top width.) Pin the new dart line from the new curved waistline to the fold, below the old dart.

Baste the darts, then baste the waistband along the curved line on the skirt top. Try it on. The back should fit smoothly over the hips, and hang perfectly straight from hips to hem. If it hikes up or sticks out in the center, then let it down a fraction. If it still droops somewhat, then take it up a little more at the waist seam.

When you have adjusted your fitting, stitch the darts and waistline seam. Press the darts toward the center inside, and the waist seam upward into the waistband. Trim off any excess material above the waist seam, and hem back the waistband as it was done originally. Press thoroughly, and it is finished.

Although this alteration requires careful attention, it is not really very difficult to do. It is one that is often needed.

A Skirt that Droops Down in the Front

For this alteration, you may have to make two small darts or pleats to absorb the extra waistline length.

Put the skirt on and pin it up as before. This time, however, you must lift up the front waist instead of the back. If the skirt already has pleats or darts in front, you do the alteration exactly the same as you did the back. If there are no darts or pleats, then make a small dart or pinch-pleat on each side, about 3½″ from the center-front. Measure across the front from side seam to side seam and divide by two to find the center. Mark this point. Match the center-

front skirt curve to the center-front waistband. Pin. Measure about 3½″ along the waistband on either side of this center-front mark, and make a small pinch-pleat in the skirt at that point so that it fits the waistband. If you prefer a dart instead of a pinch-pleat, pin out the extra material at the waistline, 3½″ from the center, crease the skirt at right angles to the waistband, and baste a small dart down to about 3″ or 4″, tapering to nothing at the bottom. Baste the waistband and skirt together, try it on, and finish as before.

13. How to Refit a Dress

WOMEN are always trying to reduce, and once in a rare while one of them actually succeeds. When she does, almost all of her dresses need taking in. So let us suppose you have triumphantly shed ten pounds, and are going to refit a dress. (Figure 13-1.)

Put on your dress and stand perfectly straight in front of the long mirror.

Always start at the waistline. Pinch out the side-seam equally on each side into a pleat, until the waist fits comfortably, and put a pin in each pleat. Then pin down each side, pinching

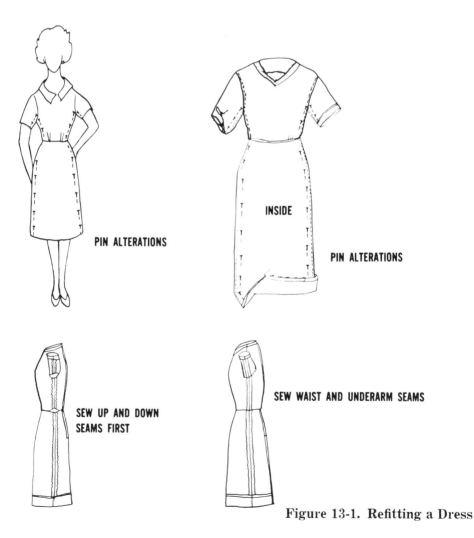

Figure 13-1. Refitting a Dress

the surplus material into a pleat with the stitching line on the outer edge of the fold, and making a nice straight line from the hips down through the hem.

Next starting at the armpits, pin a pleat down to the waist on each side of the bodice. This line will probably run at a slight angle inward to the waist, but it must be straight, not curved. Then pin the sleeve from armpit to sleeve end. Of course, if you have a friend to do this pinning for you, your fitting jobs will be much easier. If not, and you find it very difficult, try putting pins at the waist, armpit, hips and hem, then taking off the dress and pinning it all down using those measurements as a rough guide, and then trying it on. You may have to try it on and adjust it a few times, but it pays to be fussy about fitting. Remember not to fit too tightly. A well-fitted dress always has sufficient ease to allow for movement without dragging or creasing.

When the fit appears to be satisfactory, take off the dress, turn it inside out and mark all the changes with chalk or pins right on the pin lines. Remove the pins from outside, lay the dress flat on the table, and pin the changes.

Clip the threads stitching the sleeves in the dress under the armpits and the waistline seam at the right-hand side and also the sides of the hem and sleeve hem. Remove the zipper, if at the side.

Baste all the way up and down the seams. Clip the stitches in the old side seams, pull them open, and press flat. Then baste the side waistline seam and the armpits. Baste in the zipper. (If the waistline seam drags at the zipper where the side is taken in, open the seam a little way to release it.)

Try on the dress. Sit, walk, bend, and move your arms. If it is comfortable sew it up—side seams first, waistline and armpit seams second. Hand-sew the zipper and hems for better finish. Remove all bastings, press carefully and it is done.

Odds and Ends

IF you are a beginner (and even if you are not!) *never* cut a seam open —always clip the thread (about every inch) and open the seam by pulling the two sides gently apart. Then if you want to use the material in the seams, it is undamaged and usable. Besides if you cut off the old seams, you may find your new seams are too narrow, and ravel very quickly. And it is always safest to clip seams open with scissors. I do not recommend using a knife or razor blade—it is too easy to cut a hole in the fabric accidentally. And never use curved manicure scissors.

When you buy a new garment, always read the labels carefully. In fact it is a good idea to keep them in your workbox. Write on each label to which garment it refers. These labels tell what the garment is made of, and how to wash it, or clean it, and what temperature iron to use. These directions are very helpful.

When you buy material, always read the labels on the end of the bolt —they *should* tell what the fabric is made of. And if you have kept your dress labels, perhaps you can find one that refers to this same material.

When altering hems or cuffs, always rip, brush, and press down before marking the new line, wherever possible. This helps to get the new line straight. And it is easier to sew the new hem if the old crease is already pressed out.

If you get a water spot on the fabric, either from a steam iron or a wet pressing cloth, do *not* use a cleaning fluid to remove it, but let it dry; then rub the edges of the spot with your thumb nail. Rub the entire area with a dry terrycloth towel, or better still, with a piece of the same material. Most water spots can be removed without damage and without leaving marks, if done this way.

Salvage good zippers and buttons from any dresses that are no longer wearable or repairable, for use with other garments. Belts and buckles that are still in good condition can be recovered and used again.

An art-gum eraser is a good emergency cleaner for slight soil marks that are not worn into the garment when you are letting down a hem or cuff. Rub the mark with long, sweeping strokes. This will generally take off surface grime.

If your sewing machine makes an oil spot on your material, press it immediately between two pieces of clean blotting paper with a warm iron. This will lift out some of the grease.

Another way to remove an oil spot from light-colored fabrics is to rub it gently with powdered French chalk or talc powder. The chalk will absorb the oil if allowed to lay awhile, then the chalk can be brushed off. Do not use this method on black, navy or dark clothes.

Avoid using nylon linings in clothes which need much steam-pressing, because nylon melts when heat is applied.

If you prick your finger and a tiny bloodspot stains the fabric, roll a long piece of white thread into a ball and chew it for a moment. Then rub it hard over the spot. It will lift out the stain without wetting or soaking.

Very important. Watch closely as the sales clerk cuts your fabric from the bolt. Very often fabrics are cut hastily and carelessly in stores, and when you get home you find both ends are crooked and uneven, and you have to waste a lot trying to get a straight end. Sometimes you may even find you do not have enough material by the time you have straightened out both ends. Look *be-fore* it is cut off, to see whether the first end is straight on the grain. If it is crooked, then *insist* that an ample allowance be made, so that when you straighten the ends, you will have enough material. Many fabrics can be torn off the bolt, and this is much better, for it almost always tears straight on the grain. If the fabric is warped you may be able to steam-press it straight, but not always. If it is *cut* crooked, there is nothing you can do but cut it straight, and that can be very wasteful.

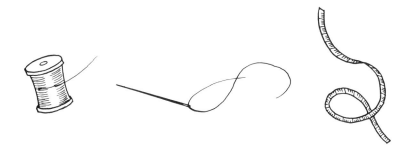

Index

Aprons, 34
Armpits, refitting of, 91

Back-stitch, 23
Band, bias, 40
Basting, 27, 31-34, 40, 47, 59, 69, 72-73, 79, 89
    equipment for, 9
    in refitting, 83, 91
Bathrobes, 22
Batiste, 21
Belting, 61, 65-66, 67, 72-73
Belts, salvaging of, 92
Bias, cutting on, 77
Binding, bias, 21, 22, 38
Bloodstains, removal of, 92-93
Bodice, reused, 50
Border
    bias, 47
    for dirndl skirt, 61-63
    to lengthen, 45, 47
Box-pleats, 47
Buckles, salvaging of, 92
Bulges, how to avoid, 83
Buttonholes
    basting of, 77
    bias-bound, 77-78
    pinning of, 77
    pressing of, 77
    types of, 77-79
Buttons
    coat, 9
    how to sew on, 11-12
    jacket, 11-12
    placement of, 11
    salvaging of, 92
    suspender, 75
    types of, 11

Chalk, 7, 18, 31, 32, 45, 69, 83, 91, (*see also* Skirt marker)
Challis, 57
Chiffon, 21
Chintz, 9, 19
Cleaning fluid, 92
Clothing
    babies', 42
    boys', 11
    casual, 34
    children's, 12, 23
    durability of, 23
    "hang" of, 17, 18
    labels in, 92
    men's, 9, 12
Coats, 21, 22
Cotton, 9, 19, 33
    glazed, 31
Crepe, silk, 57
Crewel needles (*see* Needles, types of)
Cross-grain, 17
Cross-stitching, 23-24
Cuffs, 92
Cummerbund, 57-59

Cutting
    incorrect, 93
    types of, 17
    of waistline, 69

Darts, 87, 89
Denim, 9, 33
Dimity, 21
Dress
    lengthening of, 37-49
    outgrown, 50
    refitting of, 90-91
    sheath, 17
Dresses, girls', 17

Edges
    pinked, 19
    seam-binding of, 18
    stitched and overcast, 20
    stitch line of, 21
    turned-in, 21
Embroidery, machine, 42
Equipment
    accessibility of, 8
    care of, 8
    needed, 7-8
    where to buy, 5
Eraser, 92

Fabric
    bias-cut, 77
    for border, 45
    bulky, 24
    for circular skirt, 67
    for cummerbund and scarf set, 57
    cutting of, 93
    for dirndl skirt, 61
    for facing, 38, 44, 45
    folding of, 67-68, 74
    grain of, 17
    how to buy, 93
    how to tear, 17
    labelling of, 92
    matching with seam binding, 18
    needles and, 9
    shine, 51
    shrinkage of, 31
    stretchy, 23
    width of, 57, 67

Facings
    coat, 24
    for false hem, 44-45
    hem, 38
    shirt, 74
Fasteners, 11-15 (*see also* Buttons, Hooks and eyes, and Snap fasteners)
Felt, 19
Finishing, hem-edge, 18-22
Flannel, 19
Fold, hem, 21, 22, 86
Foundation garments, 8, 18, 81
French chalk, 92

Fullness
    eliminating, 31-32
    pleating out, 32-33

Garments, care of, 92
Gathering
    avoidance of bunching, 65
    of dirndl skirt, 63-64
Godets, 30, 35

Hand-gathering, 63-64
Hand-sewing, 91
Hem-allowance, 19, 23
    of faced hem, 45
    fullness in, 31
    for lengthening child's dress, 42
    making flat, 31-32
Hem
    alteration of, 92
    back-stitching of, 23
    circular, 30-35
    coat, 24
    cross-stitched, 23
    definition of, 17
    of dirndl skirt, 61
    false, 44-45
    finishing, 18-22
    flared, 30-35
    French-style, 20-21
    godet, 32
    invisible, 34
    letting down, 37
    machine-edged, 33-35
    marking of, 18, 33, 34, 42
    overcasting, 23, 33
    pinking, 19-20, 23
    pinning, 33, 34
    seaming, 33
    stitching, 21, 23-25
    straight, 27-29
    types of, 17
    uneven, 73
    width of, 31
Hemband, addition of, 40-41
    fabric for, 40
Hemline
    adjusting, 27
    avoiding show-through, 33
    facing, 38-39
    pinning, 31, 32
Hemming, 17, 25
    accuracy in, 17
    definition of, 23
    do's and don't's, 17
    time allowance for, 25
Hem-seam binding, 27
Hem-stitches, 42
Hip closing, 69
Hooks and eyes, 14-15, 53, 65, 67, 73, 75

Iron (see Pressing)
Ironing board, 7

Jackets, 17, 22
Jersey, 23, 57

Labels, garment, 92
Lengthening, 47-49
Lingerie, 42
Linings, nylon, 92

Marking
    of hemlines, 27
    of waistbands, 70-71

Measurements
    change in, 8
    and fabric width, 67
    waist, 68
Money-saving, 5, 8
Movement, ease of, 81

Needles, 7
    care of, 8
    cost of, 9
    darning, 12
    for hemming, 23, 27
    for inserting zipper, 51
    length of, 9
    threading, 8
    types of, 7-9
Nylon, 51, 92

Oil, removal of, 92
Overcasting, 21, 23, 27, 33
Overalls, 34

Pants, 34
Patch side, 77
Patience, 5
Picoting, 75
Pinch-pleat, 89
Pin cushion, 8
Pinholes, avoidance of, 7
Pinking, 23, 27
Pinking shears, 19, 20, 34
Pins
    best type, 7
    how to store, 8
    for refitting, 91
Pinning
    of hem, 19-20
    in refitting, 81
    of waistband, 83
Pin-tuck, 42
Placket, skirt, 51
Pleating, 75
Pleating-out, 32
Pleats
    adjusting size of, 89
    hemming of, 17
    refitting and, 90-91
    show-through, avoiding, 33
    side or center-back, 29
    waistband, 86
Pressing
    avoidance of show-through, 33, 35
    avoidance of shine, 51
    of buttonholes, 79
    of faced hem, 45
    of hem, 22
    instructions for, 92
    in refitting, 91
    of seams, 83
    of skirt, 73
    with sleeveboard, 7
    steam, 32

Refitting, 81-91
Ric-rac, 42
Ripping, 25
Ruler, 69
Running-stitch, 64, 84

Satin, 31, 40
Scarf and cummerbund set, 57-59

Scissors
    for buttonholes, 77
    trimming, 19
    types of, 7
Scotch tape, 17
Seam allowance
    for dirndl skirt, 63
    for dress border, 45
    for hems, 29
    for waistband, 69, 83
Seam-binding, 18-19, 23, 33, 34, 38, 61, 67
Seams
    godet, 35
    hem-facing, 45
    how to open, 92
    narrow, disadvantages of, 92
    pressing, 47
    side, 83
Seat back, cupping of, 87-89
Selvage, 17, 65, 69
Sewing
    as hobby, 5
    how to begin, 5
Sewing box, 8
Sewing machine
    for buttonholes, 75, 77
    for hem edges, 33-35
    oil spots from, 92
    rental, 8
Sewing table, 7
Shanks, button, 11-12
Shears, dressmaker's, 7
Shifts, 17
Shine, avoidance of, 51
Shorts, 17
Show-through, avoidance of, 33, 35
Shrinkage, 31
Side-seams, distance between, 89
Silk, 34, 67
Silk pins, 67
Skirt
    attaching border to, 47
    child's, 74
    circular, 30, 67-68, 73-74
    correct length of, 18
    dirndl, 61-66
    drooping, 89
    flared, 30
    folding fabric for, 73
    gored, 30
    "hang" of, 37
    hemming, 17, 18, 74
    lengthening, 37-49
    loops to hang, 73
    measuring length of, 69
    raising, 27-35, 87
    semi-circular, 30
    setting folds in, 73
    shape, keeping of, 73
    suspendered, 50
    too loose, 81-85
    tailored, 81-89
    zipper, insertion of, 73-74
        replacement of, 51-52
Skirt marker, 7-8, 18, 27, 38
Sleeveboard, 7, 59
Slip-stitching, 22, 32, 35, 42, 45
Snap fasteners, 13, 75
Soil marks, removal, 92
Sportswear, 21
Stitching
    for buttons, 12
    for buttonholes, 77, 79
    for fasteners, 12-15

Stitching
    for hem, 19, 23-25, 28, 33, 38
    invisible, 38
    removal, 91
    running, 14, 31, 83
    of scarf, 57-58
    size of, 23
    of waistband, 69
    of zipper, 73-74
Suspenders, 75-76
Surah, 57

Taffeta, 9, 31, 38, 57
Tape measure, 7, 69
Thread
    basting, 9
    for buttons, 11
    heavy-duty, 11
    for hemming, 33
    how to cut, 9
    Nylast, 11
    where to buy, 9
Thread marking (see Thread tracing)
Thread tracing, 27, 40, 81-82, 87
Thimbles, 7
Time, 5
Toothpick, 11, 12
Trousers, 17
Tuck-trimming, 42

Velvet, 33
Voile, 21

Waistband
    adjusting, 71
    of dirndl skirt, 64-65
    fitting of, 65, 87, 89
    inserting zipper in, 51, 53
    joining suspenders to, 75
    marking of, 68-69
    pinning, 69-71
    pressing, 51
    refitting, 81, 83-84
    removing, 87
Waistline
    dipping, 63, 87
    marking, 70-71
    putting on, 68-71
    refitting, 90-91
    stitching, 72-73
Warp, 17
Water spots, removal, 92
Woof, 17
Wool, 9, 19, 23, 31, 34
Wool jersey, 57
Workbox, 8

Yardstick, 69, 83

Zipper
    center-back, 53-54, 74
    pull-tab of, 51
    in refitting, 81, 91
    removal, 83
    replacing, 51-52
    salvaging, 92
    setting in, 55
    side-underarm, 55-56
    skirt, 61, 67
    waistline, 69
Zipper tape, 51, 53, 55